MODERN MILITARY AIRCRAFT

INTRUDER

By Lou Drendel
Color Illustrations by Lou Drendel
1/72 Scale Illustrations by Joe Sewell

squadron/signal publications

An A-6E TRAM of VA-145 Swordsmen releases a load of bombs over the target. The Intruder is the Navy's best all weather attack aircraft.

ISBN 0-89747-263-2

If you have any photographs of the aircraft, armor, soldiers or ships of any nation, particularly wartime snapshots, why not share them with us and help make Squadron/Signal's books all the more interesting and complete in the future. Any photograph sent to us will be copied and the original returned. The donor will be fully credited for any photos used. Please send them to:

Squadron/Signal Publications, Inc.
1115 Crowley Drive.
Carrollton, TX 75011-5010.

Acknowledgements

U.S. Navy	U.S.A.F.
U.S.M.C.	Grumman
Boeing	Larry Mead
RADM Donald Boccker	A. W. David La Vigne
Robert F. Dorr	Robert L. Lawson
Norman E. Taylor	D. F. Brown
Shinichi Ohtaki	Nick Waters
Dr. J. G. Handleman	Ladd Wheeler
Nathan Leong	John Santucci
Jim Sullivan	George Cockle
Ted Carlson	Don Linn
Charles Howes	

(Overleaf) A bomb loaded A-6E TRAM prepares to launch from the starboard catapult of a U.S. carrier. The wing slats and flaps are fully extended to give the Intruder as much lift as possible on launch.

Introduction

The Grumman A-6 Intruder has celebrated its 30th birthday, passing even the remarkable F-4 Phantom in its length of active, front-line Naval service. Recently, Secretary of Defense Dick Cheney cancelled the A-12 program, which was over budget and years behind schedule. The A-12 was to have been the replacement for the A-6, so as a result of the cancellation, it would seem that the Intruder is destined to serve on for many more years.

The Intruder went to war again, this time in the Persian Gulf. It was mentioned often in military reports from the war zone, always describing targets bombed, boats sunk, or enemy defenses jammed. It is obviously a long way from being outdated in its ability to do the job.

The F-4 Phantom was dubbed "double ugly" by its detractors and proponents alike and a case could be made that the Intruder should be christened "triple ugly." After all, you would be hard pressed to describe the distinctive tadpole-like shape of the A-6 as "graceful" or "beautiful." In his book on the Intruder, Robert F. Dorr called the A-6 design "pragmatic," and that may be as nice a thing as you can say about the decidedly business-like demeanor of Grumman's long-lived attack bomber. But if "Pretty is, as pretty does," then the A-6 is beautiful indeed. The genius of the Intruder design is that its airframe has managed to successfully incorporate the generational development of attack avionics from the era of vacuum tubes to the solid-state digital electronics of today. The A-6 can deliver all types of ordnance regardless of shape, size and capabilities — from Second World War "dumb" bombs to 21st century "launch and leave" missiles.

When the A-6 made its first flight, Dwight D. Eisenhower was in the White House and most people still thought of Vietnam as French Indochina. A Navy Commander on flight status was making less than $9,000 per year, America had not yet put a man in space, nor suffered its first casualty of the Vietnam War. Gasoline was 35 cents a gallon, Hawaii was not a state, diplomatic relations with Cuba still existed, and most of the people who will read these words were not yet alive. Although "Culture Shock" was a term yet to be incorporated into modern lexicon, we were on the threshold of technological and social events which would seem to compress history as never before. The fact that the Intruder has not only survived these three momentous decades, but continues to thrive and will probably do so for at least another decade, is more than just remarkable. It should be cause for celebration of the genius of the designers and builders of this great airplane.

This book is a celebration of the dedication, skill and 'elan of the men who flew and fought with the Intruder. Their narrative provides the reader with insight on how the A-6 was designed and how it was used, from the beginnings of its career until 1991. In that 30 year span, one thing has not changed and that is the unique spirit of the Attack Community in which the Intruder lives. In the movie "Flight Of The Intruder," the character Jake Grafton tells a fighter pilot, "Fighter Pilots make movies; Attack Pilots make history!" They sure do, and they have been doing it and will continue to do so for many years to come in the Grumman A-6 Intruder.

Development

The designer most responsible for the A-6 Intruder is Lawrence M. Mead, Jr., who retired from Grumman as a Senior Vice President and Director of no less than seven departments including Engineering, Manufacturing, Integrated Logistics Support, Flight Test, Software Systems, Material Management and Product Training. He went to work for Grumman during 1941, and worked on all of the Iron Works fighters before being promoted to Project Engineer for the A-6 Intruder during 1957. He recounted the development of the Intruder in an address to the AIAA Long Island Chapter on 15 May 1985.

The A-6A grew from the lack of all-weather close air support during the Korean War. By the summer of 1956, an operational requirement had been developed for a STOL all-weather attack airplane which could serve for both Marine close air support and Navy long-range interdiction missions. It was to replace the Douglas AD Skyraider and do missions the A-4 Skyhawk could not.

By February of 1957, Type Specification 149 had arrived at Grumman and we put together a design team. TS-149 called for a small, two-man airplane, with a minimum of 500 knot V max, with a mission radius of 300 nautical miles for close air support, a long range interdiction mission of 1,000 nautical miles and an electronics suite which would provide real all-weather attack navigation capability. The entire weapon system was to be the responsibility of the prime contractor, rather than the historic CFE-GFE split. Single or twin engines and pure jet or turboprop were permitted. CDR Bill Ditch, Class Desk in BuAer, did an outstanding job in coordinating an extremely well-thought-out set of requirements, requirements which would still be applicable even today.

We went to work and the proposals were submitted to BuAer during August of 1957. Boeing, Douglas, Vought and Martin each submitted two designs, usually one turboprop and one turbojet. Bell, Grumman, Lockheed and North American each offered only one design. Bell's was VSTOL and was quickly eliminated. The turboprop and single engine designs also were dropped, leaving Douglas, Vought and Grumman in the finals. On 30 December 1957, we got the phone call saying we had won. I celebrated by taking the wife and four kids out for lobster dinner.

It is worth spending a little time talking about how we arrived at our winning design. During the pre-proposal period we spent a great deal of time with the operational attack squadrons gathering opinions on what was important to the attack crews. A key decision, which drove the design, was whether the two crewmen should be tandem or side-by-side. Clearly to us, opinion favored side by side, provided adequate visibility could be had to the right by the pilot. This led to the slightly staggered seats with the pilot a bit higher and further forward than the BN. This gave us better right side sight angles than either the AD or A-3. We rightly decided at the outset on two engines and Pratt & Whitney J52 turbojets rather than turboprops, for reliability and performance.

The Grumman team responsible for the development of the Intruder (left to right): Program Manager Bruce Tuttle, Chief Test Pilot Bob Smyth, and Designer and Project Engineer Larry Mead. (Grumman)

The number four A-6 on the ramp at the Grumman facility with a load of inert bombs. The aircraft has the early horizontal stabilizer and tilt-tail pipes.
(Grumman)

The prototype A-6 (A2F-1) Intruder made its first flight on 19 April 1960, with Grumman test pilot Bob Smyth at the controls. The landing gear remained down for the duration of the flight. (Grumman)

The number four prototype was later modified with the horizontal stabilizer moved sixteen inches further to the rear. The aircraft was retained at Grumman and used in a variety of test roles. (Grumman)

The number two aircraft conducts a refueling test using the Buddy Pack refueling store while refueling number four. Both of these aircraft were eventually converted to A-6B standards and issued to the fleet. (Grumman)

First class flying qualities in both the carrier and combat environment were a primary consideration. This called for excellent stability, made easier if we had plenty of tail arm for the stabilizer and fin and ample control power. Good single engine performance and control was essential. An efficient cruising machine at moderate Mach numbers was a must to meet the long-range and loitering requirements. This called for low wetted area. This quickly ruled out engine nacelles on the wings and led to the side-by-side engines in the fuselage. It also called for a moderate sweep of 25 degrees for the 1/4 chord of the wing together with an aspect ratio of at least 5.0 and modest thickness ratio of 9 to 6 percent at the tip.

The radar requirements, with two radars, one search and track, dictated a bulbous nose, which went well with side-by-side seating and the two J52s side-by-side. The radars, with the inertial platform, the crew, and the engines, wanted to be forward to get good, efficient, short inlets and help to get the center of gravity (CG) forward for a long tail arm. With the engines forward, it was possible to get the tail pipes fairly short and angled slightly out and down so that the thrust vectors went very close to the CG in both side and plan view. This made single engine trim requirements negligible and power effects small. We then moved the tail as far back as we could and still fit in the fifty-six foot length dictated by the size of carrier elevators. We built as skinny and clean a rear fuselage as we could and still hold the tail on. When you put it all together you automatically get the tadpole shape which characterizes the fuselage of the A-6.

The other driver on the configuration was weapon carriage. Somehow we had to get five bulky store stations, two engines and the main landing gear so that they would clear each other and fit within the twenty-five foot four inch width limit of the wing fold. This limit was set by passing two aircraft by each other through the fire doors on the smaller carriers. We did not want primary store stations on the folding wing panels for obvious reasons. These requirements forced the engines together and led to the ingenious landing gear arrangement which houses the wheel in the wing leading edge glove, yet gives a wide stance for ground stability.

The carrier suitability requirements for relatively low approach speeds called for an efficient high lift system for the wing, consisting of leading edge slats and double slotted flaps (later changed to single slotted modified fowler flaps) and wing spoilers for lateral controls. In searching for the right configuration, we

went through designs from 128A to finally 128Q. The mid-wings were too heavy, draggy and complicated. The low wing design was terrible from engine maintenance and removal. The 128Q became the basis for final refinement for the proposal.

The STOL requirements for 1,500 foot takeoff distance over a 50 foot obstacle (or a ground roll of about 800 feet) at a short range Marine Close-Air-Support mission weight, dictated something extra in either high lift performance or thrust, or both. Our solution to this requirement was to provide "tilting tailpipes" for the J-52 engines. By vectoring the tailpipes down 23 degrees from their cruise position, the direct lift from the thrust reduced the liftoff speed at Marine mission weight from 86 to 78 knots and the obstacle clearance distance by several hundred feet. To provide adequate low speed pitch control with the pipes deflected down, we provided geared elevators which came up as the leading edge of the stabilizer came up, but was locked out when the flaps were up. The tilt pipes were truly a "white rabbit" which contributed significantly to our win, since its weight increment penalized the basic Navy mission very little for the short field benefits to the Marines. The low approach speeds, anti-skid brakes, large tires, speed brakes and spoilers needed to make 1,500 foot short field landings also benefited Navy carrier operations.

The first contract we got in 1958 was for the start-up of design and a full-scale mockup scheduled for that fall. During this period we further refined the design. We straightened out the wing to get rid of the break in the trailing edge. This simplified the flap geometry. We eliminated the double slotted flap in favor of a semifowler single slotted tracked arrangement. We adopted a nosewheel catapult system, another first for the A2F. This added some weight, but revolutionized catapulting forever after. The most significant thing we did during that year was to firmly establish ourselves as the weapon systems manager and configure the first truly integrated airframe/weapon system that the Navy had. Bob Nafis, Gene Bonan, Dan Collins and a host of others did a tremendous job in reshaping Navy and Grumman thinking to a "system" way of thinking and away from the GFE black box mentality which preceded the A-6.

We architected the DIANE system, an acronym for Digital Integrated Attack Navigation Equipment. (Diane was also the name of Bob Nafis' daughter). It was built around the two KU band search and track radars and one of the early airborne Litton inertial platforms as primary sensors, along with the air data and doppler inputs. It was integrated with one of the early Litton airborne digital computers (using a drum memory). The cockpit display system was one of the first anywhere to provide integrated data on cathode ray tube displays for the pilot. The contact analog flight director display for the pilot was truly one of the inventions of the A-6. The synthetically generated "pathway in the sky," and the terrain clearance display coming from the phase-interferometer feature in the Search Radar, were the first steps in what has led to today's highly integrated multimode display systems throughout the world. We also had one of the first integrated weapons control and status systems in any airplane to handle the wide diversity of ordnance that the A-6 could carry.

This A-6A, assigned to Flight Test at NATC during August of 1965, carries an instrumented nose boom and a wingtip-mounted pitot tube. Both of these were later deleted when the aircraft was converted to the A-6C configuration. (U.S. Navy by PHC Kinley via Norman E. Taylor)

The number one prototype demonstrates the tilt-down tail pipes which were intended to improve takeoff and landing performance. These were later deleted as the gains were judged not worth the extra weight. The nose test probe was painted White with Red striping. (Grumman)

The integration of sensors through the digital computer allowed us to come up with a breakthrough in weapons delivery accuracy and flexibility in delivery modes, compared to previous analog fire control systems. Ballistic equations were solved with an RMS error of 1.3 mils over the entire operating range, which together with other errors allowed the system to equal or exceed the specification requirements of 10 mils for free fall weapons on the target. The computer calculated the automatic weapon release point during the pull up for a successful hit for any dive angle, pull up G, wind, airspeed, target range and velocity. Either level, low angle, or high angle release could be optioned. And all could be done under nonvisual conditions on radar significant stationary or moving targets.

Modern day improvements to the A-6 electronics suite have merely improved on the versatility of sensor, computer and display capability, but the basic system is not greatly different from the initial version. By the end of the mockup meeting in September of 1958, the configuration was pretty firm. The radome was enlarged to get both radars in. The canopy lines were improved for visibility and drag. The fin was enlarged and moved aft. We started developing a new constant speed drive package.

Shortly after that we uncovered a mistake in the cruise drag calculations (the wrong reference wing area had been used in reducing wind tunnel data). We immediately added two feet to the wing span improving aspect ratio from 5 to 5.31 and found room for another 1,000 pounds of fuel. This preserved mission radius if not specific range. This was all done with a couple of phone calls between me and LCDR C.P. (Bud) Ekas, the Class Desk Officer. We also doubled the air conditioning capacity as we got real heat rejection numbers from our avionics vendors. Also, as Newt Spiess developed the flow charts for all the Litton computer software we faced up doubling the memory capacity of computer, literally filling up the space in the cockpit between the BN's legs.

Detail drawings started into the shop and first chips were cut just about one year before first flight. The first airplane was put together in Plant 5 in early 1960. The airplane was then slow taxied at Bethpage, put on a truck to Calverton and five days later, on 19 April 1960, it made its first flight with Bob Smyth at the controls. The first aircraft had virtually no avionics in it except essential communications and navigation gear, plus a large instrumentation package for aero flight testing. A month later we held the formal Roll-out and Acceptance Ceremony at Calverton.

One of the first things we checked out after first flight was the benefits and performance of the tilting tail pipes. They performed flawlessly and the geared elevator handled the control and trim changes. After considerable debate with the Marines, however, the Navy decided that the feature was not cost-effective to retain. This was based on the fact that the tilt pipes only did any good at very light weights. At most of the T.O. mission weights the T.O. distance was only minimally improved by the tilt pipes. You could always land with the pipes up in a shorter distance than you could take off from at the heavy weights. For carrier operations, the approach speed at landing weights with tail pipes up was slow enough to suit the operators. So, out came the tilt pipe feature in all the production aircraft after number seven.

The Flight Test program did not proceed without incident. Number two aircraft, which made its first flight on 18 July 1960 from Bethpage as a ferry hop to Calverton, had a controllable fuel shut-off valve between the two main tanks in the fuselage so that we could vary the Center of Gravity during flight tests. Due to a nomenclature problem this valve was closed instead of open during this flight, and the rear tank, which was the engine feed tank, went dry and both engines flamed out just as the airplane entered downwind leg to a landing at Calverton. Ernie VonderHeyden was able to bend it around very carefully and put it down on the runway, dead stick, demonstrating the good flying qualities and an honest airplane in the process.

Just before the first Navy Preliminary Evaluation (NPE) in October, Ernie was flying a build-up flight and checking out high G with the fuselage side speed brakes extended, with power on. He noticed a sluggish pitch response. When we checked the records after the flight we found that the aerodynamic hinge moments on the slab tail exceeded the hydraulic actuator capacity and the actuator stalled for a few seconds, fortunately with no disastrous results. The extended brakes had changed the down wash pattern on the tail and moved the center of pressure inboard and forward increasing the hinge moments sharply, something we had not picked up from wind tunnel tests.

We went into a crash redesign program in January of 1961, and three months later flew with the stabilizer redesigned aft sixteen inches. We literally slid the stabilizer aft over its pivot (incidentally, almost all plastic models have the tail in the original forward position). The last major airframe changes came after NPE 1A in May of 1961. The Navy determined that the side fuselage brakes were not effective enough, both for the dive bombing mission and for work around the carrier where instantaneous drag control is needed for approach and wave-off. The only place we could find for large brakes which wouldn't buffet the aircraft, interfere with movable surfaces or weapons carriage, or give huge trim changes was where we put them, on the wing tips. These split brakes were so successful that in later A-6 models the side brakes were eliminated. The concern for asymmetrical extension was taken care of with an interlock system, which was later removed for a simple pressure tee to both wings. To my knowledge they have worked flawlessly. The last configuration change was to enlarge the rudder chord at its base, in order to give more exposed rudder area for spin recovery.

Access to the 9,300 lbst Pratt & Whitney J-52 turbojet engines was easily gained through the large access doors. The low slung arrangement of the engines made maintenance easy since most engine areas were accessible from ground level. (Grumman)

Grumman technicians work on an A-6A Intruder on the final assembly line. The aircraft to the right are C-1A Trader, carrier on board delivery (COD) aircraft. (Grumman)

The cockpit layout of an early production A2F-1 (A-6A). Although the avionics have changed, the layout remains remarkably similar in the latest variants of the A-6. (Larry Mead)

The first all-up avionics airplane was number 4, which flew in early December of 1960. The avionics hardly worked at all that first flight. Since we had not put the systems together in the lab before we flew, it literally took us weeks before we had the system working well enough to do much meaningful testing. It wasn't until the end of February 1961, that we tried the terrain clearance mode and display for the first time. It taught us a lesson for the future. The basic reliability of the equipment was poor, the environmental testing had not been rigorous enough and the lack of integration testing was disastrous. We learned a lot of things on what not to do and what to do which stood us in good stead in later years.

The first avionics NPE in November of 1961, uncovered major deficiencies in the Pilot's and BN's displays, in terms of brightness and resolution. Also, the basic system reliability problems were too large to ignore. So the first major ECP, #120, was born and approved in April of 1962, to upgrade the system reliability and the display quality. The BN's display was changed from a five inch TV display to a seven inch cathode ray tube. This had the effect of delaying the avionics BIS trials and the start of fleet training by almost a year from the original schedule.

VA-75 Sunday Punchers were the first fleet squadron to operate the A-6 Intruder. Among the first crews to fly the Intruder were LTJG Don Boecker and his BN LTJG Don Braham, boarding their A-6A on 17 February 1964. (U.S. Navy)

Airframe BIS started in October of 1962, and proceeded without much incident. In December of that year we took the A-6A, together with the E-2A, to sea for the first time aboard USS ENTERPRISE off the Virginia capes. The A-6A came away from these trials with the start of its outstanding reputation for good carrier suitability. It went on to well over 10,000 carrier landings before it had a major landing accident on the ship. During this period of Development and Acceptance testing, the airplane was sent to numerous bases for static or air display. LCDR Ekas flew it non-stop with five drop tanks, without refueling, from the East Coast to Paris. One airplane went to Thule, Greenland, to demonstrate its ability to do polar inertial navigation.

Early 1963 was an intense struggle to get the avionics system with ECP 120 acceptable for fleet use. Basic lack of reliability interfered both with the development testing and with the NPEs that followed in quick succession in early 1963. We were flying tactical missions developing the radars, evaluating ECM equipment, working on the inertial system. We made countless runs on No Man's Land off Nantucket, dropping practice bombs to work out the bugs of the release equations. We finally exceeded the 10 mil accuracy requirement getting as low as 7-8 mil CEP. We had eight to ten aircraft at Pax River all the time in either service test, weapons test, or avionics test.

Once we got Avionics and Weapons System BIS underway in March of 1963, the emphasis shifted to learning how to produce production aircraft which would work well enough and long enough to be sold to the Navy for squadron use. We were now building at two per month. Several of us, me and Dan Collins included, lived at Calverton, working the acceptance problem and keeping the Avionics BIS aircraft supported at Pax River. Finally, on October 10, 1963, #32 aircraft was accepted and delivered to the fleet as the first operational squadron airplane. Despite the basic reliability problems, the A-6A was such a vast step forward in delivery range, ordnance versatility and payload, all-weather search and track capability, and general utility that the Navy couldn't get them fast enough. As we know they went on to an enviable record of performance in Vietnam in the mid-1960s.

From the very outset, we designed the A2F-1 (A-6A) for versatility and growth potential. We didn't skimp on the aerodynamics, the strength, or performance. The system architecture was adaptable to modernization. The very first proposal brochure spoke to alternate versions, such as ASW, Reconnaissance, ECM. The airplane was used as a Tanker almost from the outset, long before we developed the KA-6D. We started study work on an ECM version in late 1960, with Lew Scheuer as Project Engineer in my office, and by August of 1961, we started active work on the A2F-1Q, which made its first flight on 21 February 1963, as the EA-6A. This aircraft was converted from the second A2F-1 prototype with modified electronics from the A-6A. From this airplane we went on to A-6B, C, D, E, KA-6D, EA-6B in its several versions, and now we are in the midst of another major upgrade to both systems and airframe in what will be the A-6F. This has all been possible because the original mission requirement and airframe and system design was well-thought-out in the first place.

Don Boecker

I have had the great good fortune to claim as a friend one of the most impressive military aviators of the past three decades. Don Boecker and I were classmates in grammar school. I went on to a military high school and a short, undistinguished stint with the 82nd Airborne. Don attended Naperville Community High School, went on to Annapolis and an outstanding career in the Navy.

As these words are written, Don is a Rear Admiral (two star) and Commander of the Naval Air Test Center at Patuxent River, Maryland. Don opted for the attack community during flight training and, after two Med cruises with VA-76, flying A-4C Skyhawks, was assigned to VA-75 as one of the first operational pilots of the A-6A Intruder. His recollections of that tour, including taking the Intruder into combat for the first time, were first published in my "A-6 Intruder In Action" (1975). Since that book is now out of print, it seems appropriate to reprint the story here...it is that exciting and important to the history of the Intruder.

LT Don Boecker (left), LT Don Eaton (center) and CAPT Duke Windsor, CO of USS INDEPENDENCE after the successful rescue of the two A-6 crewmen from enemy territory. (RADM Don Boecker)

I checked into VA-75 Sunday Punchers during 1963. At the time, VA-75 was still an A-1 Skyraider squadron, but was scheduled to become the first fleet A-6 squadron. There were about 110 people assigned and the squadron still had three A-1s which had not yet been transferred to other squadrons. I was assigned the job of Personnel Officer, which meant that I had to check in all new people and check out all of the A-1 personnel who were going to other fleet A-1 squadrons. This was quite an undertaking, since we retained very few of the original VA-75 complement. In addition to transferring the A-1 personnel, I had to check in the 330 new A-6 personnel who had been drawn from various jet attack squadrons throughout the fleet. Since we were the first A-6 squadron, and the A-6 was the first really all-weather attack aircraft the Navy had, the squadron received some of the best people in the Navy.

The first order of business was a maintenance school, followed by an examination. We then began our flying with VA-42, the A-6 Replacement Squadron, where I was joined by my Bombadier Navigator (BN), Don Eaton, now also a Rear Admiral. We were all thoroughly impressed with the A-6 and enjoyed the flying immensely.

The squadron finished the RAG in February of 1964, and was assigned to Air Wing Seven (CVW-7), aboard USS IN-DEPENDENCE (CVA-62). At that time the USS INDEPEN-DENCE was still in the Mediterranean, completing a seven month cruise. Consequently, we did our qualifications (CAR-QUALS) aboard two other ships. Our day CARQUALS were accomplished aboard USS SARATOGA (CVA-60) and night CARQUALS were done aboard USS FORRESTAL (CVA-59).

After our CARQUALS, we began an intensive program of full-system bombing at Tangier Target. Tangier Target is an old freighter, which had partially sunk in the Chesapeake Bay, off Tangier Island (80 miles north of Norfolk). The Mayor of Tangier Island called the target spots to the aircrews who did their bombing there. One of the memorable events of this period was the dropping of the 100,000th bomb on Tangier Target. Pete Easton, one of our pilots, did the job, and was rewarded with a helicopter trip to the island and a ceremony put on by the Mayor, complete with cake to mark the occasion.

During the Fall of 1964, we moved aboard USS INDEPEN-DENCE for a two week cruise up to the World's Fair at New York City. We were to showcase USS INDEPENDENCE, her air wing and our brand new A-6 squadron. During our stay the officers of VA-75 were feted at a cocktail party on top of the Time-Life Building, which was sponsored by Grumman. Grumman also arranged tours of the city for us and a three day golf weekend. After eight days in New York, we sailed, spending five

days at sea while returning to Norfolk. During this time we conducted air operations and sharpened our skills.

For the four months following this short cruise, we operated out of NAS Oceana, conducting training flights to Tangier Target and various low-level missions into the mountains of North Carolina, Virginia, West Virginia and Tennessee. During this time VA-75 became a real family. We had a weekly happy hour gathering every Friday and twice a month the wives would join us for dinner and dancing afterwards.

Early in 1965 we moved aboard USS INDEPENDENCE for a short cruise to the Caribbean. We were notified that we would be departing for WestPac in May. During this cruise we intensified our training, practicing weapon delivery on the island of Viecas, which is between Saint Thomas and Puerto Rico. The bombing of North Vietnam had begun in earnest and we anticipated going to war, so the training took on additional intensity.

Upon our return to Norfolk, preparations got underway for our WESTPAC cruise. We were given daily briefings on some aspect of the cruise, either on the latest intelligence or on some personal aspect of going to war. We got twelve brand-new aircraft, right off the assembly lines with all the latest modifications installed.

We left on 10 May and I'll never forget that day. It was one of the real sad experiences of my life. All of the crew's families lining the pier to wave, some of them seeing each other for the last time. One of the sad personal incidents of that leave-taking was related to me by my wife when we returned. She was standing on

Don Boecker and Doug Bibler alongside their A-6A, which carries fifty-seven Black bomb mission symbols on the fuselage, along with a "Tonkin Gulf Yacht Club" insignia. (RADM Don Boecker)

the pier with the wife of our Executive Officer, CDR Mike Vogt. As we pulled out, his wife turned to my wife and said she had the feeling that she would never see her husband again. Her feeling proved all too accurate, as CDR Vogt was later killed on a mission over North Vietnam.

We steamed down to Puerto Rico, where we held an ORI (Operational Readiness Inspection), simulating an actual at-sea war period. Upon completion of the ORI we spent two days and nights at Saint Thomas, giving everyone a chance at liberty before the long voyage around the tip of Africa and through the Indian Ocean.

Our next stop was Singapore. During our stay there, the officers of VA-75 had an ADMIN ashore at the Regal Hotel, which was an elegant holdover from the days of British Colonialism. Eight of us in the squadron were avid golfers and by working through the Embassy, we obtained permission to play the Royal Singapore Island Country Club, which was later featured on Shell's Wonderful World of Golf. We had four Malaysian caddies, probably about fifteen years old. I'll never forget the first hole on that round. We walked to the first tee and the yardage marker said 370 yards. There was a big valley between the tee and the green though and it looked more like 280 to me. I took out my driver and hit one of the best shots I had ever hit. The ball hit short and rolled right up on the green! I then proceeded to sink a thirty foot putt for an eagle. Well, from that point on I was King to those caddies...they had never seen that done before. I didn't shoot that well for the rest of the round...82, I think...but that first hole made my day.

We left Singapore and steamed up to Cubi Point in the Philippines, where we began our last tune-up before going into combat. It had been about a month since we had last flown, so we were a little rusty and were grateful for the chance to fly between Singapore and Cubi and to drop practice bombs on the SPAR, which is a target towed behind the carrier. We got our last-minute briefings and, prior to leaving Cubi, all crewmembers who were going to fly over Vietnam were required to go through a one day survival school. The instructors for this course were former Filipino guerrillas and they schooled us in the art of finding food in the jungle and evading the enemy. This one day school supplemented the one week course we had all gone through in the States.

The second squadron to take the Intruder into combat was VA-85 Black Falcons. Prior to their Vietnam cruise during 1965, the squadron worked up on USS KITTY HAWK (CVA-63). Behind the A-6A is another Grumman carrier aircraft, an E-2 Hawkeye. (Grumman)

Finally we reboarded USS INDEPENDENCE and headed for Vietnam. Enroute we were thoroughly briefed concerning the dos and do nots of flying over Vietnam. The next day we flew our first combat missions. We were on what came to be known as "Dixie Station" and we flew into South Vietnam. An Air Force FAC, flying an O-1, called us in on an enemy bunker complex. He fired his smoke rockets, then instructed us to bomb 50 meters to the north. We rolled in and dropped on his target, which we never really saw. There was no anti-aircraft fire. After we pulled off target, he gave us a bomb damage assessment and credited us with destroying the bunkers. We headed back to the ship. I don't know what I had expected, but this was certainly anti-climactic. I thought; "If this is what combat is like, it's sure not going to be very exciting!" I didn't know how wrong I was, but I didn't have long to wait to find out.

We spent about three or four days on Dixie Station, then moved north to begin the war in earnest. It was about the first of July, 1965. I remember vividly the 4th of July mission that I flew. I had five Mk 84 2,000 pound bombs on my aircraft and they were really decorated for the occasion!. It didn't take the ordnancemen long to pick up on the time-honored custom of decorating our bombs with uncomplimentary salutations to the enemy. I think the favorite was, "Ho Chi Minh is a Son of a Bitch!"..It became so popular that it was usually abbreviated to HCMIASOB...after all, we never expected them to be able to read the message anyway. But the bomb loaders often added to it. One I remember is, "Mary and Jane from Norfolk send their greetings to you...HCMIASOB!"

On 14 July, we were number two in a flight of two A-6As assigned to crater a road near Sam Nua in Northern Laos. My flight lead was LCDR Bill Ruby. My BN was Don Eaton. We were carrying five Mk-117 500 pound bombs, one on each station, because of a shortage of bombs. The target was several hundred miles from the ship. Shortly after take-off and rendezvous, LCDR Ruby's aircraft weapons system failed and he passed the lead to us. We led the flight to the target at 25,000 feet, arriving in the target area about 1800.

We armed our bombs and rolled in on the target. The bombs were set to become armed four and a half seconds after leaving the aircraft and to detonate on impact. The target elevation was 3,500 feet above sea level. We rolled in at 18,000 feet and at 9,000 I had a good target picture, so I pickled as briefed at 5,500 feet AGL. There was an immediate heavy explosion under the starboard wing. The port wing dropped about ten to fifteen degrees and the starboard fire warning light came on. I told Don I was

securing the right engine and pulled the throttle back while pulling out of the dive. I went to 100% power on the port engine and began to slowly climb out while we made a damage assessment. Within seconds we lost 2,000 pounds of wing fuel and there was a rapid pitch-up of the right wing, so we assumed that one of the bombs had gone off either on the rack, or immediately after release. We looked back to the wings and couldn't spot any holes in either of them, but fuel was streaming heavily from the trailing edges of both wings. We were doing rapid mental calculations, trying to figure how much fuel we had, how fast we were losing it, how long it would last with the one engine at 100%, where the nearest divert field was, where the nearest tanker was...when suddenly it all became academic. The port engine fire warning light came on! This was followed by a rapid loss of hydraulic pressure. The control stick locked in a ten degree nose-down, port wing low position. I told Don that we were going to have to get out. That was seconded by LCDR Ruby, who transmitted, "You're on fire! EJECT!" I went to slap Don on the leg to tell him to eject, but he was practically gone by then. I waited a couple of microseconds, then pulled the face curtain myself.

Since we were below the altitude that the barostat initiates the automatic sequence when we ejected, there was no delay at all in the beginning of that sequence and before I knew what was happening I was hanging in my chute. I looked around and saw our aircraft, in a gentle turn, diving toward the ground. I also saw Don and even though he had ejected before me, I was passing him due to the difference in our weight (I'm a 200 pounder, while he weighed about 140). I looked back at our aircraft, just in time to see it fly into the side of a mountain. There was the initial impact, then a tremendous secondary explosion that appeared to totally demolish the wreckage.

The ground was getting closer and, much to my consternation, I saw that I was heading right for a small village. I could see people in the village pointing up at me and I thought they were going to shoot at me as I descended. I sure didn't want to land anywhere near any people, for obvious reasons, and I began to frantically pull on my parachute risers, trying to steer clear of the village. I didn't seem to be able to influence my glide path though, and just when it looked as though I was going to hit right in the middle of the village, a gust of wind caught me, drifted me over a little hill and I landed about 200 yards to the southeast. Just before I landed, I could see armed soldiers running out of the village in my direction.

The area I landed in was marshy, with bull rushes about ten feet high. My parachute caught in a 20 foot tree, but I made a soft

This scene is played out each time an Air Wing returned from deployment. Whether combat or not, the families of Naval Aviators realize the dangerous business their men are engaged in, and the expressions of relief and joy are universal. (David F. Brown)

landing in the weeds. I immediately released my rocket-jet fittings, took off my helmet, and prepared to get out of there.

In the meantime, Don Eaton was not fairing so well. In the early model A-6As, the ejection was through the canopy. The top of the seat incorporated a canopy breaker that was supposed to shatter the canopy. This, combined with the greater cockpit pressurization, would cause the plexiglass to explode outward, making a hole for the aviator to go through. Apparently something didn't work quite right for Don, because his hands were severely bruised on the way out of the aircraft. His opening shock was also heavy and his pistol broke loose and banged him hard in the face. To make his misery more complete, he landed in tall grass, which caused him to misjudge his altitude and he hurt his back with a hard landing on hard ground.

I had to make some quick decisions on what to take and in which direction to run. I looked around and saw that Don was going to land on the other side of large, grassy hill to my south. That direction was out...I'd never get over that hill before the enemy caught up to me. To the North there was another hill, but unlike the grass covered hill to the south, this one was a tangle of thick jungle undergrowth. That looked like the best bet for cover and concealment. I grabbed my survival equipment out of the parachute seat pan, and in the process accidentally actuated the nitrogen bottle that blows up the one man life raft. Frantically, I picked up the raft and, with the super human strength born of fear and adrenaline, ripped it apart and threw it aside. I have

An A-6A of VA-85 makes an arrested landing aboard USS KITTY HAWK. The deck crewman to the right will signal the pilot when the aircraft has come to a complete halt and will assist in disengaging the tail hook from the wire, if necessary. (Grumman)

A-6A Intruders of VA-85 on the hangar deck of KITTY HAWK. The aircraft in the foreground is the 90th A-6A built. VA-85 carried the squadron patch on the fuselage behind the cockpit. (Grumman)

unsuccessfully tried to duplicate this feat several times in subsequent years. Finally, with my survival equipment in hand, I took off for the hill. I crossed a little stream and plunged into a rice paddy. I didn't get ten feet into the paddy before I realized that I would never get to the other side fast enough...the mud was just too thick. I doubled back to the dike and took off around the paddy. I crossed a heavily traveled foot path and was into the jungle. I started up the hill, my mind spitting out the things I had learned in survival school. I was careful not to unnecessarily break any branches and I tried to leave the bush as it had been before I came through.

After about a hundred feet of this, I came to what looked like an ideal hiding place, an animal den, and I burrowed into the hole, pulling underbrush over me. I barely had time to catch my breath before I heard about ten or fifteen men beating the brush, and hollering back and forth to each other in their native tongue. They had found my chute and were actively searching for me! We had ejected about 1830 local time and I knew that the sun went down about 1930. It was now about 1900...I figured that if they didn't find me before dark, I would be able to put some more distance between us during the night. I stayed put, really sweating it out...thinking that it would never get dark. It finally did though, but the voices persisted in their search until 2200, when they finally faded off into the distance.

I stayed hidden for another two hours, then decided to move to a spot farther away from the village. I took off my torso harness and G suit, removed my compass, knife, and other survival

Loaded with Mk-82 Snakeye 500 pound bombs, an A-6A of VA-85 roars off the number one catapult aboard Kitty Hawk for a combat mission over Vietnam. The aircraft has a Yellow rudder with five Black eagles on the trailing edge. (Grumman)

equipment, buried the harness and G suit in the animal den, and started to move away. About that time, I heard some strange, almost mechanical sounds. The noises were coming from the valley below me and they almost sounded like crickets to me. Don also heard them from his position and he described them as sounding like squeaky fan belts, or possibly a truck with bad valves. We never figured out what they were, and they only lasted about a half an hour, but they appeared to have been some sort of signals from man to man.

I started off to the northwest, aiming for the top of the hill. It took me the better part of three hours to make it. The undergrowth was extremely thick and I had to move on my hands and knees part of the time and even on my stomach at other times. I wanted to get to the thickest part of the jungle, and that's where I ended up! The trees at the top of the hill were too high to allow a helicopter rescue and I felt sure that the helicopters would be there at first light, so I made my way back down the hill about 20 or 30 yards to a point where the underbrush was quite thick, but at the same time, the trees were not so high. I stayed there the rest of the night, unable to sleep...I was still pretty well pumped up, and it was extremely cold because of the high elevation.

About 0500 the next morning I heard an aircraft overhead. It was still dark, and the aircraft was way up high, so I thought it was probably a commercial aircraft. But when the sun came up at 0630, I looked up and there was a C-54 circling overhead. The night before I had checked out my survival radio, making sure that the battery was connected and that it worked properly. The homing beeper was so noisy though that I was afraid to use it, so when I spotted the C-54 I called them. No answer. I called repeatedly while it circled, but still no answer.

About 0715, four A-1 Skyraiders showed up. I called them, but got no answer. Finally, on the off-chance that I might be sending, but not receiving, I asked them to rock their wings if they heard me. They started rocking their wings almost immediately, and I felt a whole lot better right away! As soon as the sun got over the mountain, I used my signal mirror to show them my location. I was later warned about this by some of my rescuers, who told me that whenever they saw flashes on the ground they assumed that it was ground fire and attacked the area of the flashes. Fortunately, I had told them that I was using the mirror.

About 0815 two H-34 helicopters showed up and began searching for us. Although the A-1 pilots had my position spotted, the helicopters were having a real rough time finding us. One of them was searching an area of the hill below me and I was frantically telling him, "I'm at your six, slightly high...back here!" He had just turned around and started for me when the enemy opened up on him with a heavy machine gun. He took a hit in his main fuel cell and started streaming fuel. I hollered for him to clear out and he did. The other helicopter went with him, escorting him back to a safe landing site.

Just after the helicopter was hit and limped off to a safe area, I heard a man approaching my position. I got down on my stomach and hid in the thick undergrowth. I watched him walk to within eight feet of my position and I was petrified! I thought for sure that he had seen me! My heart was pounding so loud that he should have been able to hear it! Either he saw me and was afraid to take any action, or he missed me because of the thick brush...I'm still not sure which, but I'll never forget the feeling of being hunted by many men with guns, with death or capture imminent. It's a feeling that is difficult to describe...except to say that you're damn scared! I was glad that I had made the decision not to carry a sidearm. I think I would have been tempted to shoot him, then call on the radio for the helicopter to get me out...and of course, they could not have, and it would have been all over for me.

Now things really got tense. I knew that I should move to a more open area to make the rescue effort easier when the helicopters returned, but I couldn't. I could hear people all around me, searching the jungle. I decided that if the helos didn't come back, or if they couldn't get me that day, that I would wait and move again that night. I think the longest three hours of my life were that morning while I awaited the return of the helicopters. Two of our A-6s had arrived on station and I tried calling them. They heard me, but of course I couldn't know this since I had no receiver. Don Eaton had a receiver, but no transmitter, so he could hear what was going on, but couldn't tell anyone where he was. Fortunately, he was in a more open area and the enemy was concentrating their search efforts in my area. The A-1s were joined by some Lao T-28s and USAF F-105s, and they remained on station all morning relieving each other periodically to return to base for fuel, I became convinced that morning of the effectiveness of the A-1 in the rescue role. Many other aircrew also found out how good the A-1 was.

About 1130 the helicopters returned. I was able to transmit to them and as soon as the A-1s and T-28s heard their acknowledgements, the planes began to attack a little village about 80 to 100 yards from my position. I hadn't realized that I was so close to the enemy. They started a large fire with their guns and rockets...lots of secondary explosions, so evidently the enemy had plenty of ammo stored in the village. The fire was really

The third Intruder squadron to see combat was VA-65 Tigers aboard USS CORAL SEA. This A-6 is loaded with MERs on each pylon for a total of twenty-eight Mk 82 Snakeye low drag 500 pound bombs. (Grumman)

going strong, and it had me a little worried, because the jungle was pretty dry in that area. Luckily, the wind was blowing the fire away from me and it never caused a problem. While the A-1s and F-105 Thuds were strafing and bombing, the helicopters were searching for Don and I.

Don had done a lot of moving that morning, in spite of his many hurts. At the time he thought they wouldn't get to him, since he didn't have a transmitter. As soon as he heard the helicopters return, he ran to the top of a small hill and lit a smoke flare. They didn't spot the first one, so he lit another and waved it over his head. One of the T-28s spotted it and dove for him. It suddenly occurred to him that the T-28 pilot might have mistaken him for an enemy soldier and he hit the deck. But the T-28 pulled out over him, dropped a wing, and as Don looked up, the pilot waved to him. Don waved back, and the T-28 rocked its wings. Shortly after that, one of the helos landed nearby and picked Don up.

In the meantime, I was calling the helicopters, trying to give them my position. I was in deep underbrush and was sure that they were going to have a tough time spotting me, so I decided on what I considered to be a last-ditch maneuver. I called to them and told them that the next time they came over me, I would light a smoke flare. Shortly after that, one of them came over and I lit the flare. One of the crewmen spotted me right away and waved...but the chopper kept right on going! I couldn't imagine what had gone wrong. I later learned that the crewman who spotted me didn't have a headset...he was a Thai door gunner who didn't speak English well enough to make the pilot understand that he had spotted me. Now the A-1s were really plastering the village, and I was getting very nervous about this. I decided to move to a more open area regardless of the danger. I began running...really crashing, I guess would be more accurate ...through the jungle. I got to an area that had a big canopy tree, which was an ideal landmark. I called the helo and told him that I was directly up the hill from the big canopy tree, and he came over my position almost immediately.

They hovered over me and started reeling out the cable with a horse collar attached. The rotor downwash was terrific...bending all the brush over, and blowing the sling around. The sling kept getting caught in the trees and it seemed like an hour before they got all the cable out. When they finally did get it all out, it was about three feet above me, and downhill...and they couldn't get any closer to me because of the tree. I was going to have to jump for it. I dropped all my survival gear and made a desperation leap for the sling. I just managed to get one arm through it, and found myself being dragged through the edge of the tree and out over the valley. It took them about three minutes to hoist me aboard, but in the meantime I was hanging in the horse collar by one arm, holding on to that wrist with the other hand with a death grip, while the helo was flying about 60 knots and climb-

Loaded with twenty-two 500 pound bombs, this A-6A of VA-196 Main Battery operated off USS CONSTELLATION (CVA-64) during 1968. The ship was on Yankee Station in the Gulf of Tonkin for most of its cruise. (U.S. Navy)

This A-6A of VA-65 has a MER on each outboard station and the centerline station for a total of eighteen 500 pound bombs. The aircraft is on the starboard catapult of the USS CORAL SEA (CVA-43). The A-6 was the first aircraft to employ the nose-tow catapult attachment, which has greatly simplified catapult operations. (Grumman)

ing for altitude. The troops on the ground were shooting at us, and the A-1s were diving under us, attacking them. What a show! I was at least 2,000 feet in the air over the valley floor before they finally pulled me aboard. The first person I saw was Don Eaton huddled in the rear of the cabin. What a welcome sight! We were like a couple of kids on Christmas morning, congratulating each other on our good fortune. They took us back to a safe area and we caught an Air America flight to Udorn, where we were debriefed. After debriefing, we thought about taking liberty, but we were just too worn out after our ordeal.

The following day we were flown back aboard USS INDEPENDENCE by the ship's E-2 Hawkeye. CAPT Duke Windsor, skipper of the INDEPENDENCE, had planned a reception for us, complete with brass band and cheering shipmates. We were the first in the air wing to go down, and everyone was elated that we had been rescued. On the day after our return to the ship, they flew us to Cubi Point in the COD so that we could call our wives. The wives had been messaged when we went down, and again when we were rescued, but we wanted to reassure them that we were in good shape.

The day after our return from Cubi Point was an important one on the USS INDEPENDENCE. I was squadron duty officer, and was not flying, so I had a chance to observe most of the visit of the Secretary of Defense, Robert MacNamara. Mr. MacNamara attended the briefing for the Alpha Strike that had been planned for that day against the Thanh Hoa power plant. Commander Jerry Denton, the air wing Operations Officer, was leading the strike and the Secretary of Defense acted as Catapult Officer to launch Jerry's A-6.

Unfortunately, we lost Jerry Denton and his BN, Bill Tschudy, on this mission. They were the first to roll in and were hit almost immediately. They ejected and were captured. Jerry Denton landed in the center of the Thanh Hoa River. He released his parachute and attempted to swim underwater to evade the enemy, but was captured a short time later by several enemy soldiers in a small boat. Bill Tschudy landed in the middle of a courtyard and was captured as soon as he touched down. We were all saddened by this loss...our first in combat over the North. CDR Denton had been scheduled to assume command of VA-75 the very next day. CDR "Swoose" Snead remained our Commanding Officer until word came down from Washington to promote CDR Mike Vogt to the post. (Authors note: Jerry Denton remained a POW until 1973, and Don Boecker was his official escort officer upon his return. Denton was elected Senator from

Alabama in 1980, after retiring from the Navy as a Rear Admiral).

On the day following this mission, I resumed flying. My first mission was to act as a tanker aircraft for the A-4s which were performing RESCAP duties in the futile attempt at recovering Denton and Tschudy. I was up for three hours and refueled several of the A-4s. They gave it a good try, but the North Vietnamese had long since captured our squadron mates.

We lost our third A-6 six days later. LCDR Deke Bordone and his BN LTJG Pete Moffet were hit at low altitude. The airplane started a slow, uncontrolled roll and they were forced to eject in a nearly inverted position. Both were severely injured. Fortunately they were only down about four hours before the helicopters got into the area and rescued them. Pete Moffet was so severely injured that he never again flew an ejection seat airplane. Deke was more fortunate. After a period of convalescence, he returned for another cruise, this time with VA-85, and flew many combat missions. He was eventually promoted to Commanding Officer of VA-75 and later served as CAG-3 on the USS SARATOGA, leading strikes against the North during the heavy bombing just prior to the end of the war.

We had lost three airplanes and two crews in twelve days on the line and the Navy was alarmed. They conducted an investigation, the upshot of which was to stop daylight VFR bombing in the A-6. It was just too expensive (about six million dollars per copy at the time) to allow it to be used for high risk, low value, targets. The only exception to this rule was when the A-6s were used to lead the Alpha Strikes. These were large strikes in which the entire air wing was committed. Our three lost airplanes were replaced with brand-new A-6s which had been flown across the Pacific. The crews were not replaced and as a result the rest of us got a lot more flying time. We had started with fourteen crews and twelve airplanes. Now we were down to twelve and twelve, so we began flying double launch flight cycles. The flights now lasted three hours instead of the customary hour and a half. The normal flight then would consist of a two plane section taking off for strikes on pre-planned targets, with targets of opportunity as back-ups. The missions would last three hours, two of which were over North Vietnam. We liked to have two planes on these missions because if one got into trouble, he knew the other was in the vicinity and could radio for help or spot the position of the downed airplane. We got a lot of night flying on these missions.

After about 30 days on Yankee Station, we pulled back to Cubi Point for some R&R. I always enjoyed Cubi because of the fine golf course they had, and the excellent Officers Club on the hill. The little town of Olongapo, which was adjacent to Cubi, turned into quite a prosperous city. Thousands of Philippinos had migrated to it, just to get the dollars from the sailors and marines on liberty. And the money was really spent after these long at-sea periods!

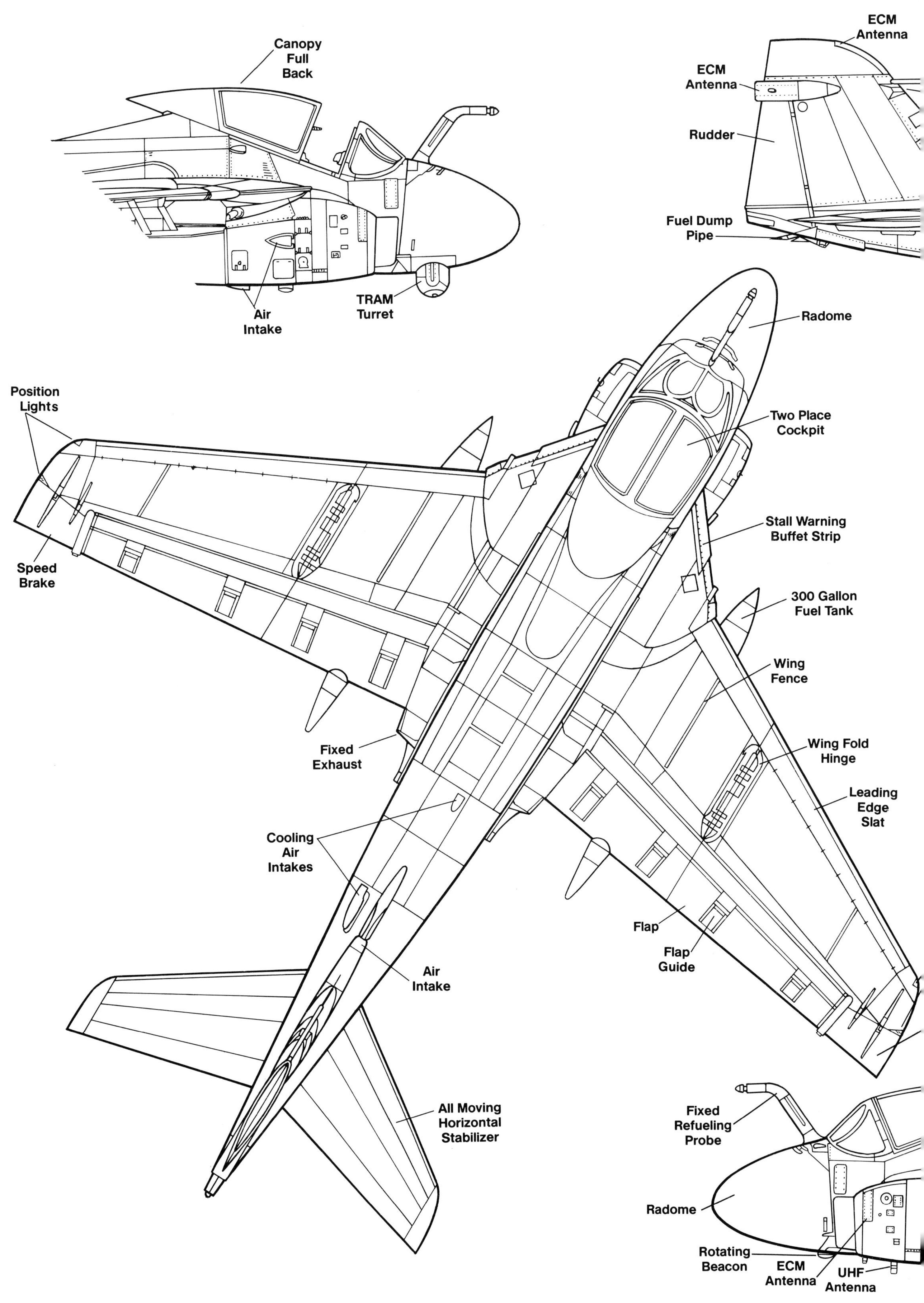

Canopy Full Back
Air Intake
TRAM Turret
ECM Antenna
ECM Antenna
Rudder
Fuel Dump Pipe
Radome
Two Place Cockpit
Stall Warning Buffet Strip
300 Gallon Fuel Tank
Wing Fence
Wing Fold Hinge
Leading Edge Slat
Flap
Flap Guide
Position Lights
Speed Brake
Fixed Exhaust
Cooling Air Intakes
Air Intake
All Moving Horizontal Stabilizer
Fixed Refueling Probe
Radome
Rotating Beacon
ECM Antenna
UHF Antenna

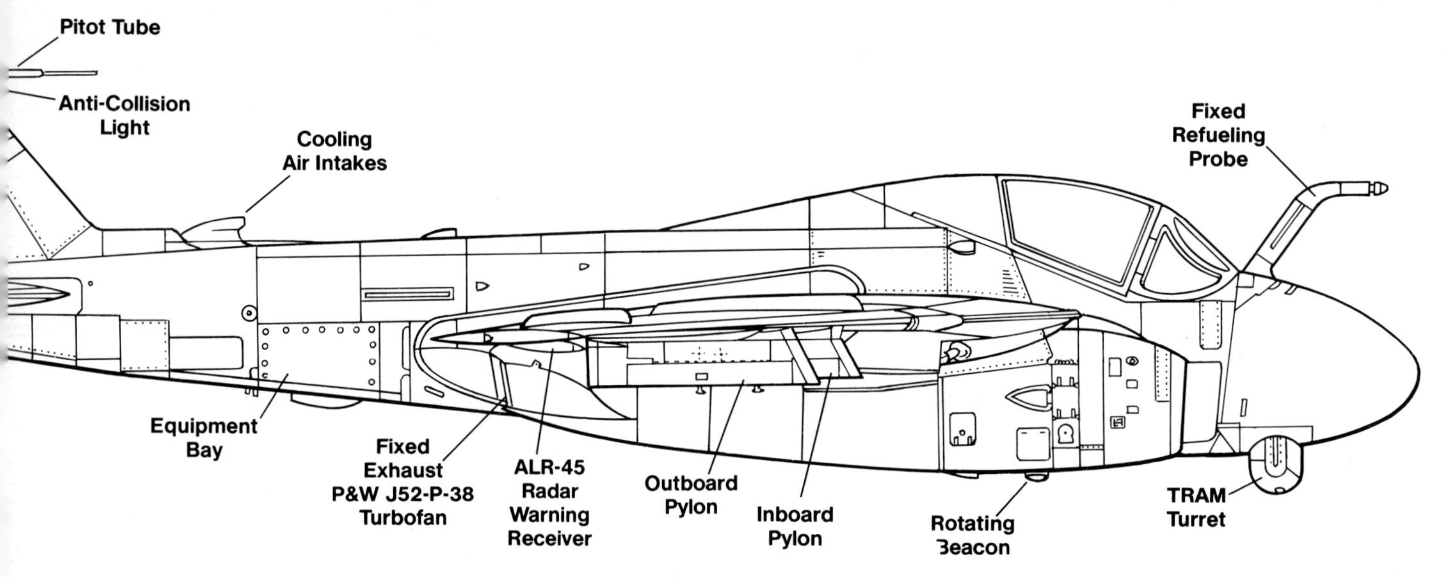

Missiles

AGM-65 Maverick
(4 Wing Stations)

AGM-84 Harpoon

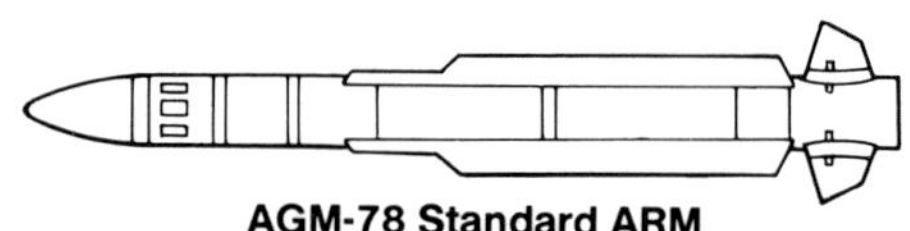

AGM-78 Standard ARM

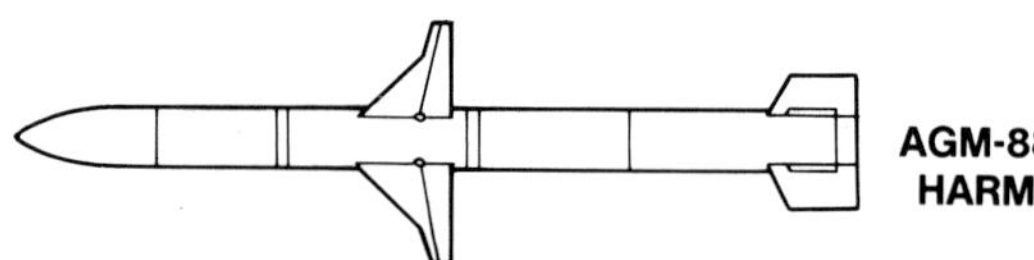

AGM-88 HARM

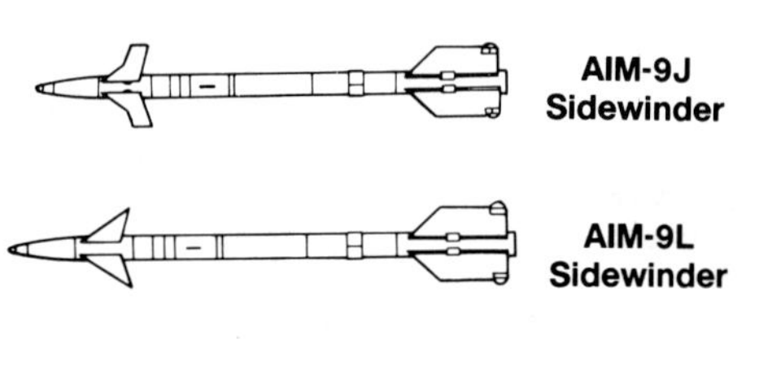

Specifications

Grumman A-6E Intruder

Wingspan . . . . 53 feet
Length . . . . 54 feet 9 inches
Height . . . . 16 feet 2 inches
Empty Weight . . . . 25,980 pounds
Maximum Weight . . . . 58,600 pounds
Powerplants . . . . Two 9,300 lbst Pratt & Whitney J52-P-8 turbofan engines.

Armament . . . . Up to 18,000 pounds of ordnance.

Performance
  Maximum Speed . . . . 653 mph
  Service ceiling . . . . 44,600 feet
  Range . . . . 2,378 miles
Crew . . . . Two

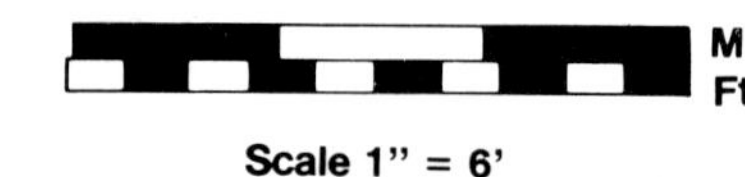

Scale 1" = 6'

A-6A

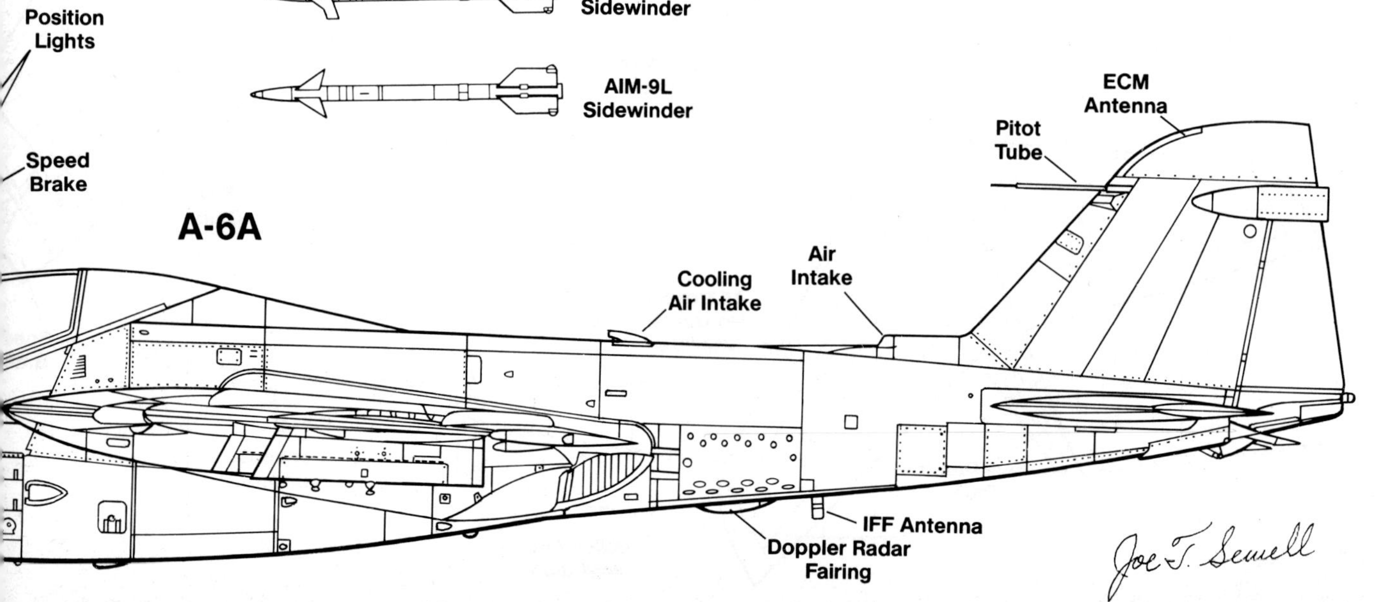

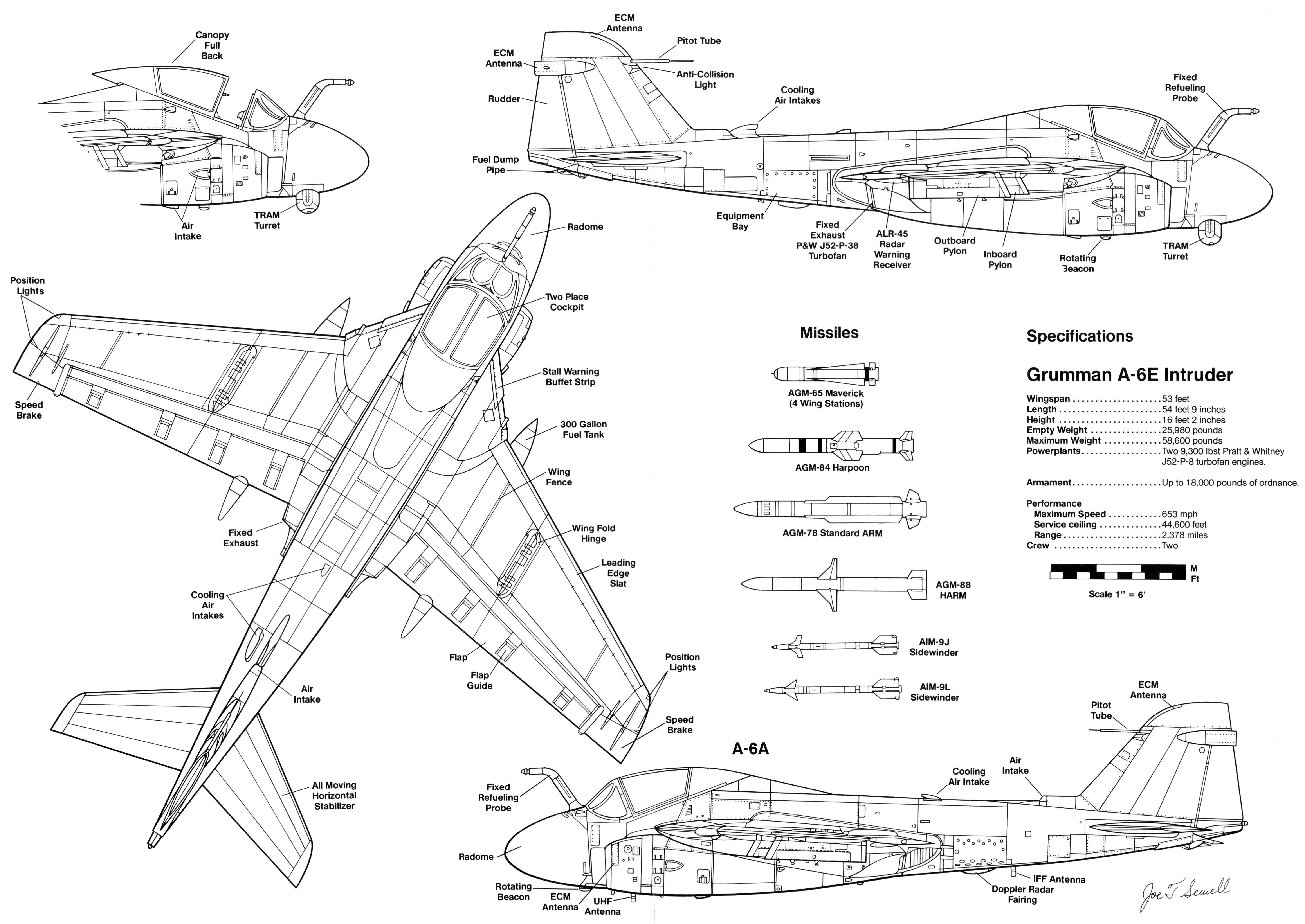

Canopy Full Back
Air Intake
TRAM Turret
ECM Antenna
ECM Antenna
Rudder
Pitot Tube
Anti-Collision Light
Cooling Air Intakes
Fixed Refueling Probe
Fuel Dump Pipe
Equipment Bay
Fixed Exhaust P&W J52-P-38 Turbofan
ALR-45 Radar Warning Receiver
Outboard Pylon
Inboard Pylon
Rotating Beacon
TRAM Turret
Position Lights
Speed Brake
Radome
Two Place Cockpit
Stall Warning Buffet Strip
300 Gallon Fuel Tank
Wing Fence
Wing Fold Hinge
Leading Edge Slat
Fixed Exhaust
Cooling Air Intakes
Flap
Flap Guide
Position Lights
Speed Brake
Air Intake
All Moving Horizontal Stabilizer
A-6A
Radome
Rotating Beacon
ECM Antenna
UHF Antenna
Fixed Refueling Probe
Cooling Air Intake
Air Intake
IFF Antenna
Doppler Radar Fairing
ECM Antenna
Pitot Tube
Missiles
AGM-65 Maverick (4 Wing Stations)
AGM-84 Harpoon
AGM-78 Standard ARM
AGM-88 HARM
AIM-9J Sidewinder
AIM-9L Sidewinder
Specifications
Grumman A-6E Intruder
Wingspan . . . . .53 feet
Length . . . . .54 feet 9 inches
Height . . . . .16 feet 2 inches
Empty Weight . . . . .25,980 pounds
Maximum Weight . . . . .58,600 pounds
Powerplants .Two 9,300 lbst Pratt & Whitney J52-P-8 turbofan engines.
Armament .Up to 18,000 pounds of ordnance.
Performance
Maximum Speed . . . . .653 mph
Service ceiling . . . . .44,600 feet
Range . . . . .2,378 miles
Crew . . . . .Two
M
Ft
Scale 1" = 6'
Joe T. Sewell

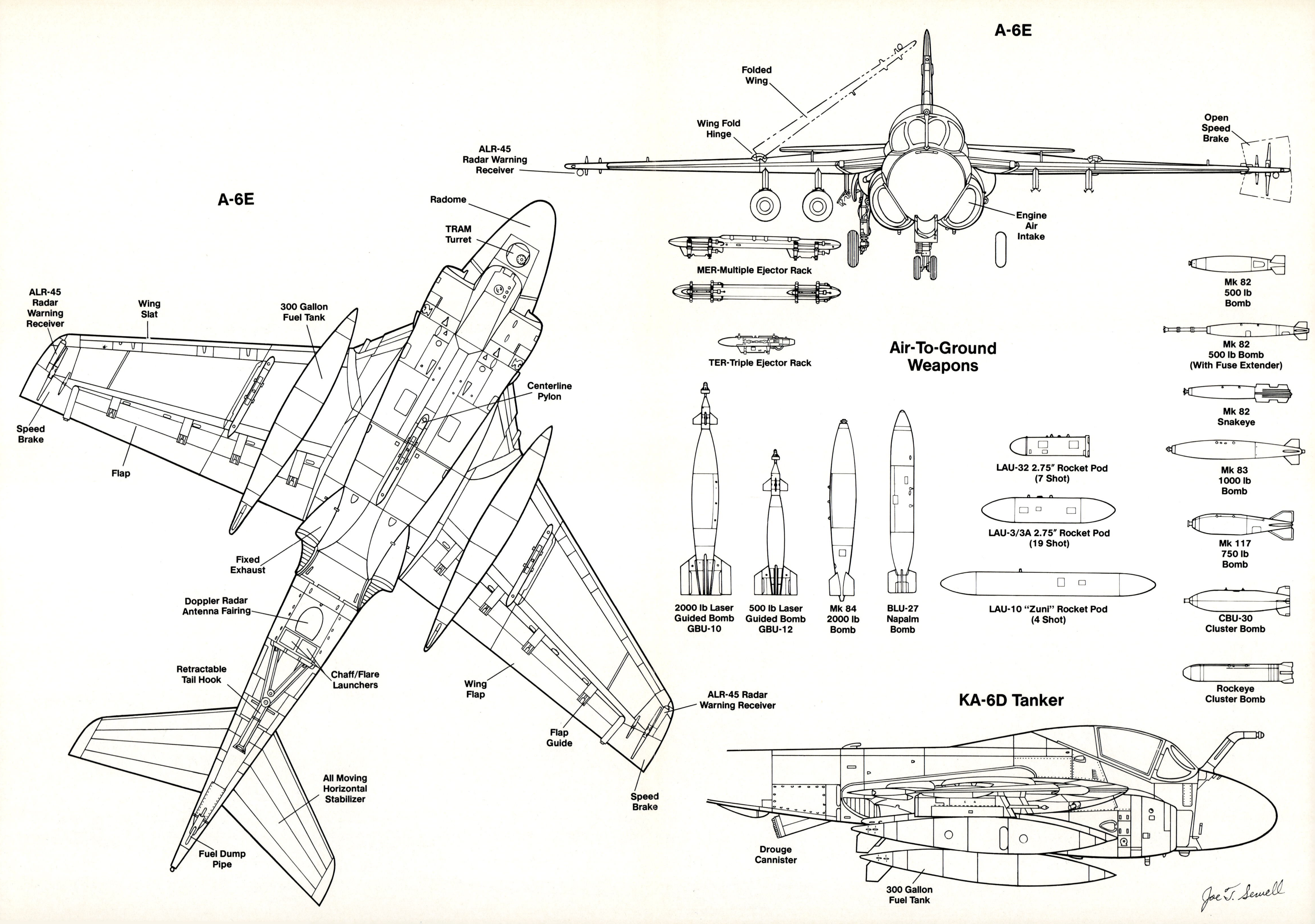

A-6E
A-6E
Folded Wing
Wing Fold Hinge
ALR-45 Radar Warning Receiver
Open Speed Brake
Engine Air Intake
Radome
TRAM Turret
ALR-45 Radar Warning Receiver
Wing Slat
300 Gallon Fuel Tank
Speed Brake
Flap
Centerline Pylon
Fixed Exhaust
Doppler Radar Antenna Fairing
Wing Flap
Retractable Tail Hook
Chaff/Flare Launchers
Flap Guide
ALR-45 Radar Warning Receiver
Speed Brake
All Moving Horizontal Stabilizer
Fuel Dump Pipe
MER-Multiple Ejector Rack
TER-Triple Ejector Rack
Air-To-Ground Weapons
Mk 82 500 lb Bomb
Mk 82 500 lb Bomb (With Fuse Extender)
Mk 82 Snakeye
Mk 83 1000 lb Bomb
Mk 117 750 lb Bomb
2000 lb Laser Guided Bomb GBU-10
500 lb Laser Guided Bomb GBU-12
Mk 84 2000 lb Bomb
BLU-27 Napalm Bomb
LAU-32 2.75" Rocket Pod (7 Shot)
LAU-3/3A 2.75" Rocket Pod (19 Shot)
LAU-10 "Zuni" Rocket Pod (4 Shot)
CBU-30 Cluster Bomb
Rockeye Cluster Bomb
KA-6D Tanker
Drouge Cannister
300 Gallon Fuel Tank
Joe T. Sewell

After Cubi, we were back on Yankee Station for another thirty-five day line period. Fortunately, VA-75 did not lose any people during this period, but the air wing lost an A-4 pilot and an F-4 crew. After a liberty period in Hong Kong, we resumed night bombing. On our first night back, I had two flights totalling about six hours. The reason for the two missions in one night, was that I had been scheduled as the "go" bird on the first mission that night, which I flew. Upon my return, I was briefed as a standby on the next mission. I had no expectation of flying that one, but when the number two A-6 went "down" on the deck, I was taxied forward, launched and flew the mission.

The most terrifying night of my life occurred the night I flew a mission with LT Doug Bibler. This was my first night flight after being rescued, and Don Eaton was still not medically fit to fly. The two hours we spent over North Vietnam were relatively uneventful...I think we bombed a truck park or something. But I'll never forget the return to the ship.

Ordinarily, a night landing aboard the carrier is not too scary. But on this occasion, the ship was steaming through a thunderstorm. It was the only cloud within twenty miles, and the ship was right under the middle of it. I proceeded inbound and at ten miles from the ship, I was hit with a terrific case of vertigo. I would have bet a million dollars that I was flying 90 degrees right wing down. I knew better, of course, from my instruments, which indicated I was flying straight and level. I told Doug I had vertigo and asked him to monitor the attitude instruments to make sure I didn't succumb to the vertigo. I approached the ship for my landing and at three miles I started my let down under Carrier Controlled Approach (CCA). At three quarters of a mile, I was told to take over visually and call the ball (I should have been able to see the "meatball" of the mirror landing system at that distance). I looked out my windscreen and could not see a thing. I decided to take my own wave-off and added power. Suddenly, the island structure of the carrier loomed in front of us. We flew right by it, barely missing a collision. I flew upwind into the bolter pattern, the vertigo still raging. I told Doug that I would try one more pass and if we did not get aboard, I would divert on my own to Danang. Normally it is the ship's Captain that makes the decision whether or not the airplane is to continue or divert. But my vertigo was so bad, I felt that we might not live through more than one more pass.

I got my instructions from CCA to turn downwind and when we were directly abeam the ship I looked out the port side of the canopy and spotted it. We continued our approach. I turned on the windscreen air full blast, and this seemed to clear some of the heavy rain from the winscreen, because I could just barely make out the ship. I still could not see the ball and the LSO talked me through the entire landing. I don't remember which wire we caught, but we did get aboard. I taxied forward, shut down, opened the canopy and climbed down. I got on my knees and kissed the deck, even though it was still raining like the prover-

bial cow on a flat rock. As I went down to the ready room, I was still shaking...it was the worse experience I ever had aboard ship, and I attribute our safe landing to Doug Bibler's calm coaching during the approach.

About the middle of September, one of our aircraft was due for a maintenance cycle and Don Eaton and I were picked to ferry it to Cubi. We manned the aircraft, taxied to the catapult, added 100 percent power and launched. I reached up to raise the gear as soon as we were airborne, and the A-6 was racked by a tremendous explosion. I went right to the instruments, but could not see any sign of trouble. In the meantime, the gear had come up and we started to lose altitude. The flaps were still down and their added lift kept us airborne. It was about five o'clock in the afternoon and the sun was shining onto the instrument panel...so I did not see the starboard fire warning light. When I looked back, I saw the light and told Don Eaton that I was shutting down the starboard engine. I told Don which engine because in times of stress, pilots have been known to shut down the wrong engine, and having your BN monitor your actions is a good backup. I shut down the engine and continued to climb until we had enough altitude and airspeed to raise the flaps. We tried to contact the ship, but for some reason the radio decided to quit working at that time, so we could not talk to anyone.

I spotted an A-3 tanker orbiting the ship and decided to join up on him in the hope that I might be able to communicate our problem to him via hand signals. Our receivers were still working, so I could hear what was being said, but could not talk to him. I joined up on the A-3 and began giving him all kinds of hand signals...asking him if we were on fire, to look me over, were the engines damaged? None of these got through, I heard him tell the ship that he had an A-6 on his wing that wanted to land immediately. I shook my head vigorously no...I was too heavy to land. Finally, Don hit on the idea of getting his survival radio out and calling the A-3 on the guard channel. It worked and we were able to tell him about the fire warning light and shut down engine. He looked us over and reported that the entire starboard rear engine cover and tail pipe had been blown off the aircraft. He called the ship and reported he problem. Since the A-6 had not yet made a single engine landing aboard a carrier, the Captain decided that we should divert to Danang. We made an uneventful flight and landing at Danang, and after looking at the aircraft, I realized just how lucky we had been to get back safely.

We spent the night at Danang and were treated to a big beer party by the Air Force. About 0300 an F-8 pilot who diverted to Danang came in and told us that he had heard that a Flying

A pair of bomb loaded A-6A Intruders of VA-35 prepare to launch from USS AMERICA for a 1971 combat mission over Vietnam. VA-35 is the oldest attack squadron in the Navy and the fourth oldest Navy squadron of any kind. (Grumman)

An A-6A of VA-35 Panthers on the starboard catapult just seconds before launch. The aircraft is carrying a load of Mk 82 low drag 500 pound bombs configured with standard fins. (Grumman)

Aces (our call sign) aircraft had been lost over North Vietnam. Between worrying about who had been lost, the heat, two VC rocket attacks and the primitive quarters (tents) I didn't get much sleep that night. The next morning the COD came in to pick us up and we learned that the squadron commander, Mike Vogt and his BN, Red Barber, had been lost and there was almost no hope that they survived. CDR Warwick, who had started the cruise as number three on the squadron seniority list, was now the commanding officer and we were down to eleven crews. They replaced the lost aircraft, and a week later we got a replacement crew fresh from training.

The scariest missions for me personally were the daylight Alpha Strikes, in which about twenty-four aircraft hit the same target at the same time. The one that stands out the most was the strike against the Kep highway bridge. Four A-6s led the mission and this was the first time I saw a SAM missile fired. They shot thirteen SAMs at the strike aircraft. The CO of one of the F-4 squadrons said one passed so close to him that he could read the serial number on the side. I remember rolling in on the target...each A-6 carried five 2,000 pound bombs, so after the first A-6 had dropped, the target was pretty well obscured by smoke and dust. We got the bridge, but there was a dike about 200 to 300 yards down river that the supply trucks could drive over, so it was really no big deal to the North Vietnamese...and we lost an F-4 and A-4 on the mission. We flew right over Kep airfield and could see the MiGs on the ground...but they did not come up.

We had five or six of those air wing strikes during the last part of the cruise and, as I said, they were the scariest missions for me personally. I would much rather fly an A-6 alone, at night, than go on an Alpha Strike. The results were outstanding, but our losses were pretty heavy too. The North Vietnamese would fire every conceivable type of ammunition at us, in abundance, and everything that goes up must come down. I would have hated to have been on the ground during one of those strikes.

After an inport period in Japan, we had our last line period. It was pretty uneventful and we were all counting the days until we headed for home. We stopped in Cubi on the way home to offload our A-6 spares, which were to be picked up by VA-85 on USS KITTY HAWK, who would be making the second A-6 combat deployment.

Our home coming was on 10 December 1965 when we launched the entire air wing from 150 miles at sea, joined into a long trail formation and headed for NAS Oceana. We overflew the base at 500 feet, split up and landed. Of course, all the wives and families were on hand to greet us, so it was a great home-coming. When I reflected on what I had seen during our five and a half months on Yankee Station, I decided that there was no chance of the war ending in the next five years, if we continued to run it in the manner in which I had seen it run. Unfortunately, my estimate was all too correct.

Don Boecker graduated from the U.S. Navy Test Pilot School in June of 1967 and was assigned to the Naval Air Test Center. He ran the test program on the A-7D/E for two years, then went on to VA-42 at NAS Oceana. He later served three years as XO and CO of VA-85 aboard USS FORRESTAL, followed by a three year tour as A-6E class desk officer at Naval Air Systems Command. He was assigned as XO of USS SARATOGA for a year and a half, then returned to Washington for a tour in the Office of the Under Secretary of Defense (R&E) in the Tactical Warfare Branch. He made two Med cruises as Commanding Officer of USS CONCORD (AFS-5) before being reassigned to Washington as Head of Aviation Plans and Programs (OP-508) for a year before moving to Deputy Director, Aviation Plans and Requirements Division (OP-50B) for two years. In July of 1987, he was selected for Rear Admiral and assigned as the Commander, Naval Air Test Center.

He has been awarded two Legions of Merit, the Defense Meritorious Service Medal, the Meritorious Service Medal, six Air Medals, two Navy Commendations with combat V, the Combat Action Ribbon, a Navy Unit Commendation, the Meritorious Unit Commendation, the Navy Expeditionary Medal, and several Vietnam decorations. He is married to the former Gay Lanier Scott of Winter Haven, Florida and they have six children.

LTC A.W. David LaVigne on his return from Vietnam during 1968. (A.W. David LaVigne)

LTC A.W. David LaVigne, USMC

...is a native of Worcester, Massachussets. He graduated from Assumption College (AB Degree) during 1948, studied Medicine at the Georgetown University School of Medicine and was engaged in research (biochemistry) in Endocrinology when the Korean War began.

He enlisted as a Naval Aviation Cadet and earned his wings during 1952. He flew the F6F-5, F4U-4 and F9F-5 before joining VMF-311 for combat missions out of K-3, Korea, during 1953. Later in that tour, LaVigne was dispatched to the Gulf of Tonkin to join COMPHIBGRU ONE, which was engaged in the mass evacuation of (then) Northern French Indochina. The group consisted of forty MSTS ships. While with COMPHIBGRU ONE, he worked with the French Expeditionary Units and Naval Forces, serving in Intelligence functions ashore and afloat and as Aide and Interpreter to Commander, U.S. Naval Forces.

LaVigne returned to CONUS to join attack squadrons then flying the AD-4 and A4D-4 before joining 3rd Battalion, 8th Marines for an infantry tour in Battalion Operations. LaVigne later flew assault transports in a variety of assignments including logistic support of the 6th Fleet and deployed units in Lebanon in 1958. He returned to Vietnam during 1962 flying logistic support of expeditionary units and serving also as G-2 (A), 3rd Marine Expeditionary Brigade in Northern Thailand.

While a Major, LaVigne served as Executive Officer of Marine All-Weather Attack Squadron 533 (VMA AW 533). During 1967 he returned to Vietnam for the third time as CO of VMA (AW)-242 during its 1967-68 combat tour. He also served there in Marine Air Group 11 Operations and as OIC of its Air Combat Operations Center at Danang, RVN. During this tour, LaVigne flew an additional 222 combat missions, 200 of which were in the northern Route Packages, including nine "Super Barrels" in Route Packages V and VI,

where he qualified as one of the early "River Rats." He earned eighteen Air Medals, two Single Mission Air Medals, the Bronze Star with combat "V" and the Distinguished Flying Cross.

He later served as Project Manager of the OV-10 and on the AV-8A Procurement Project, and also was engaged in the sales of military aircraft to foreign governments.

Retiring in 1971, LaVigne earned his Juris Doctor Degree (with honors) from the National Law Center, George Washington University during 1973 and became a partner in the Worcester, MA, law firm of Wilson & Bourgeois, concentrating in the areas of Civil Litigation, Commercial Law, Probate and bank operations matters. LaVigne later reduced the scale of his practice to that of his own office, retiring from the full time practice of law during 1988, to spend more time sailing his cutter 'The Oscar D' out of New England ports.

His account of combat missions and conditions in Vietnam for Marine A-6 crews during 1967-68 follows:

There is something special about the role of Attack aviation. That is where the action is and I recognized that years ago. Having cut their teeth in fighters, a good many aircraft drivers also realized, at one time or another, that they could spend a whole military career without ever having engaged an enemy aircraft. In that instance, it was stretching a point to call oneself a fighter pilot. In Attack, an aircraft driver can really do some good. Making a rail cut, taking out a train or a bridge, an ammunition storage dump, a fuel depot, a truck park, or enemy airfields...these are the targets that all Attack and Fighter pilots seek. Because fighters do not usually have enemy aircraft to engage, they must pick up Attack as a secondary mission...perhaps in aircraft not ideally suited for the mission. That is why some of us prefer the role of Attack. Fighter or Attack, all of our aircraft drivers did a fine job, largely as a product of their attitude towards the enemy: KICK THEIR ASS!

From my days ashore in North Vietnam after the fall of Dien Bien Phu and at the start of the mass evacuation during 1954, I could still visualize the vast number of concrete fortifications and gun emplacements built by the French, and probably earlier occupants, up in the Red River Delta. I continued to remain impressed by my early exposure to the French in the field, their paratroopers...tough as nails...wearing red berets, their colonial troops (Les Colons) who wore the blocked, billed cap (Les Cepis), the French Navy corvettes in the river and harbor approaches, and the French Foreign Legion (La Legion Etrangere), whose camps were in such horrible places, as somewhat dried-out, but still muddy, rice paddies and who were thankful for some decent American C-rations.

And there was wire, tactical wire everywhere and more acres of it further in the interior towards Hanoi. Wire especially related to the concrete block houses and watch towers with the aiming slits and overlapping fields of vision and overlapping fields of fire along the coast highway. I often wondered whether they were still being used during the American air campaign, and whether we may have dented any of them. The French

VMA (AW)- 224 was formed on 1 November 1966, at Marine Corps Air Station Cherry Point, N.C. The squadron deployed to Vietnam the following year, along with VMCJ-1. (LaVigne)

would readily admit at that time that although they held the country by day, as soon as the sun went down they held only up to the immediate perimeter defined by their own tactical wire, that short distance well within the range of their machine guns, so that at night they could "tire, tire, au feu" (fire machine guns) and, in the morning after it got light, pick the bodies off the wire.

An A-6 crew at Danang flew mostly alone, mostly at night, mostly north of the DMZ in the lower route packages and frequently on the deep penetration missions in route packages V and VI. The bird was sometimes accompanied part of the way on the "Rolling Thunder" missions by F-4s for fighter cover when MiGs were expected, and hopefully accompanied by Marine ECM birds (VMCJ) to jam North Vietnamese SAM and AAA acquisition and fire control systems which blanketed the northern route packages.

Returning from these missions in the early hours meant eating breakfast after Intelligence debriefing and then going to bed, so that the usual work-day started later, around 1000, when you ambled over to Operations, lifted up the canvas cover on the classified target-depiction chart, checked the flight schedule and found out who was assigned to what target and whether it was "your night in the barrel."

The A-6 guys who flew "Rolling Thunder" applied the term "Superbarrel" to any target, usually in Route Package VI, which Intelligence briefed as being defended by over 600 AAA guns within a radius of eight miles of the target, numerous smaller caliber visually-directed weapons sites, ten to twenty overlapping SAM missile sites and a possibility of MiG intercept. The target could therefore be expected to be close to Hanoi.

Generally, if the MiGs were up, the AAA and SAMs were down. And if the MiGs were not up, you could expect a very warm reception from the AAA and SAM batteries. We didn't worry much about MiGs at any distance from the target, figuring that our Marine F-4s (VMFA-122) or our Air Force brethren would keep them off our back, or that we could run them out of range of their home base when we were headed back to our base. Close in to the target, however, MiGs simply had to be outflown...that is down on the deck, among the ridges and valleys in the black of the night where they could not follow.

SAMs were more of a problem, although if you could pick them up visually, soon enough, you could usually out turn them. The attack and egress courses usually put you through or past ten to twenty or so overlapping twenty mile radius rings before your aircraft made "feet wet" or before you got out of range of missiles in the "Bullseye" (Hanoi) area.

It was when the night was really black and you were running your attack or egress in the soup or heavy rain (which we loved) and then the flashing red MISSILE WARNING light lit up the cockpit...it was then that you puckered because your couldn't see the missile and had to guess at its lift-off point and trajectory (later aircraft had better equipment which gave the crew azimuth information). When you thought the time was right, you yanked

Loaded with 1,000 pound bombs, an A-6A of VMA (AW)-242 Bats heads for a target in North Vietnam. Marine Intruders operated from bases in South Vietnam against targets in both North and South Vietnam. (USMC)

on a lot of Gs and did a few wild turns and, if you were lucky, the warning light went out. If the SAM detonated below you and flipped you over on your back at 800 feet above ground level (AGL) with a full bomb load, like it did to Lou Abrams (Navy Cross), then you had another problem. Not too many folks can recover like Lou, take another missile going in, fight it, then go on to drop all ordnance on target, take on another missile on the way out, and still bring the airplane back to fight another day.

It was the AAA and AA that really got your attention most of the time because there was so much of it. Yet, those Gooks had taken that course in economy of management and they didn't waste many rounds. During and after an attack which drew intense fire, the sky usually went black again in just a few minutes. This was particularly noticeable to A-6 crews, who came in alone and drew concentrated fire, as opposed to multiple aircraft strikes where the ground fire reaction was diluted among several aircraft. But A-6 people liked it that way and it exposed only a few of their aircraft to fire on any given night.

A disturbing aspect of deep strikes was that the enemy could watch us and track the flight for a long time before the actual attack run began. Although it was the black of night and hopefully it was raining or overcast, which naturally diminished the threat from visually directed weapons, the Red warning lights rimming the console told us we were being watched. Mission profiles included low-high-low or high-low-high. Either way, at some time you were visible to enemy radar. Breaking ground at Danang, of course, you are low and might stay low going "feet wet" to stay out of enemy radar if the target was in the lower route packages. You would stay "feet wet" and low until crossing the beach for the attack.

But in the upper route packages, the mission profile called for cruise climb to altitude for best fuel economy until you were deep in "indian country," then you could drop down into the valleys and between the ridges to evade their acquisition radars while coming up on the initial point (IP) to commence your attack. Usually the "low" was a descent down to 800 feet AGL up to and beyond the IP, finally climbing to above 1,500 feet for the bomb drop (1,800 feet was even better). They had tracked you for a long time, and they waited for you with up to 600 guns and then gave you the full blast for a couple of minutes.

During the climb to altitude, passing Route Package I on your way north, the console began to display a flashing Red warning light, indicating that enemy search radar pulses were bouncing off your nose. As you went deeper, you picked up "left wing warning," then "right wing warning," and finally "tail warning." When that happened, you knew you were in "indian country" because all the warning lights were blinking at you

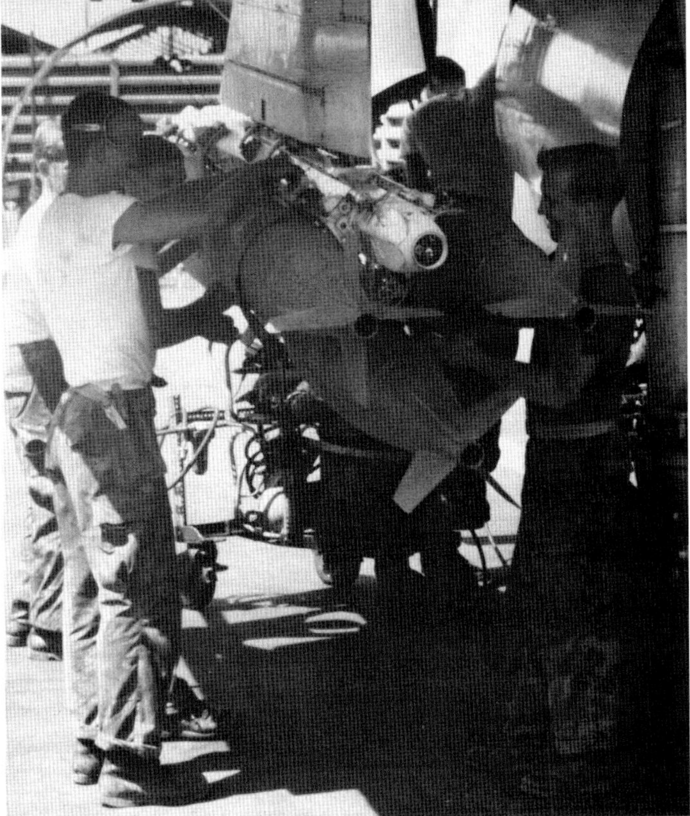

Ordnancemen loading bombs on Multiple Ejector Racks (MERs) aboard an A-6A in Vietnam. Early bomb loads included World War II bombs which were fitted directly to weapons pylons. These bombs armed themselves within a second and at least three Intruders were lost because the bombs went off early. (USMC)

simultaneously, indicating that the enemy was tracking your progress. Before reaching your IP, one or more of the warning lights would go from blinking to steady, indicating that they were no longer searching, but were now locked on to you, computing your position, altitude, and course and feeding the information into their fire control systems in preparation to firing. And when you heard that high-pitched whine in your headset, you knew that something exciting was about to happen.

Occasionally, you would get a reaction some distance from the IP, but that was not the usual case. The sky stayed Black, the ground was as Black as the inside of an inkwell and it all seemed real quiet. Dropping down on the deck to minimum terrain clearance, you are running hard, ballistics computer all set, cursors tracking, the IP showing up on the scope and moving down the scope, you are doing a fast instrument scan checking all altimeters (barometric and radar) and terrain clearance presentations...five seconds to IP, ninety-five seconds to target. As you clear the IP, the throttles go forward to full military power with a hard turn to the attack course, dropping out of 3,000 feet (clearing the ridge by less than 300 feet), down to 800 feet AGL for the attack, then pop up to above 1,500 for bomb release. Now, coming out of a hard turn, aircraft accelerating, rolling wings level for the final attack run, ninety seconds to target — ALL HELL BREAKS LOOSE!!

Tremendously heavy AAA and groups of searchlights which appear to move in unison and locked on to the aircraft as it jinks left, right, up and down. The streams of tracers coming up at you makes you feel like you are standing at the bottom of Niagra Falls looking up at the torrent coming down on you. Like a firehose following you around, the volume of fire tells you that if you stop jinking, they've got you. The violent maneuvering "dumps" the platforms and the ballistics computation and steering. The BN says, "I'm going manual, hold her steady! (Easy for him to say, he has his head buried in the scope and doesn't see what you see outside the aircraft). Only seconds to drop, but it seems like hours...then comes the rumble as the ballistics mechanisms start kicking off the bombs, and as the drag comes off the bird, you feel her accelerating and respond-

ing better as she picks up speed. In the mirrors that rim the cockpit canopy you can see the ring of airbursts round the aircraft and see the streams of tracers from the visually-directed weapons which are shooting into the middle of the ring of airbursts. But you scoot away at max power, dropping down below a protective ridge and, when the time is right, zoom up to clear the mountains on your way back down the western track. Almost immediately the ground and the sky would go Black again, usually only a couple of minutes having elapsed, but more exposure than that was bad for your health.

If you took a MiG bounce up there and went to max power to fight or evade it, you sucked up so much fuel that you had only about two to four minutes to engage. Beyond that, you did not have enough fuel to make it home and you would have to try to make it to an airfield in Thailand, or try to find a friendly tanker for a drink on your way back. Not that easy when it is Black and maybe stormy and you just finished wrestling with a bandit. Plugging in under those conditions takes "cool" man.

And once in a while, if the mission took a missile on the way out, turning around to engage it also made you short of fuel for the return trip. Fuel and evasive maneuvering required some planning and technique. Les Widick was one of those guys. Flying a deep penetration mission in a MiG and SAM environment, he struck his target under intense AAA fire and then fought a missile on the way out. Short of fuel, he found and coolly plugged into a tanker in that Blackness about 0200 in the morning and then brought the aircraft back for the next day's launch. Not bad Les, what else can you do?

There were other good missions. A favorite was the Armed Recon Mission, which looked for targets of opportunity. It was coveted because it allowed the "sportsmen" to go up there in the deeper packages and truly hunt and destroy. The track was eastern, up the coast, sometimes staying low over the water for the lower route packages, but usually higher for the more distant missions. Checking in with the picket ships (Red Crown) off the coast gave you tactical contact, but although they watched the progress of your mission in their Combat Information Center (CIC), they rarely came on the frequency. But when they did, it was worth listening to them.

After checking in with the ship one night, we turned west from over the water in the vicinity of route package four and were about to cross the beach into RP IV when the BN said; "We got movers" (moving targets). Sure enough, the Moving Target Indicator (MTI) gave a presentation which looked like a truck column moving south along the coast highway. The BN fine-tuned his presentation and set up the ballistics computer while I set up for a run along the length of the column for best effect.

The first drop was run to the north, followed immediately after release by a 90/270 timed-turn (a 90 degree turn, followed by a 270 degree turn in the opposite direction will position the aircraft on a reciprocal heading and, if timed correctly, will result in a return to the same target area.) The first turn was to the right, so as to come right back on an aiming-heading for the column for a second run heading south. There was another strung-out drop of about 5 bombs, followed by another 90/270, this time to the left. We changed altitude for the third run, again to the north. It was a great hunter-killer mission...the kind you

An A-6A Intruder of VMA (AW)-242 takes off from Danang Air Base for a combat mission during 1967. The aircraft is carrying a total of twenty-two 500 pound bombs. (USMC)

With its wingtip speed brakes deployed, an A-6A of VMA (AW)-533 Hawks makes an arrested landing at Chu Lai during December 1967. The MOREST arresting gear and SATS catapult system made operations with heavy bomb loads possible from Chu Lai. (USMC)

always hope for. We had a beautiful string of targets and were pounding them with good accuracy and effect. There were a lot of secondary explosions and many fires were started. Then Red Crown announced, "BANDITS. Airborne out of Bullseye." followed by their position and heading, which made it clear they were headed in our direction, and closing.

The target was so great that we hated to break off the attack, so we decided to make one more run to dump our remaining bombs. While we were rolling out of the 90/270 on a southerly heading, Red Crown announced, "BANDITS 8 MILES AND CLOSING FAST!" We rogered, pickled off the remaining ordnance, went to max power, streaking south and down to pick up speed. Then we got the tail warning light, followed immediately by the lock on warning and we were in trouble. We made a hard, diving turn and broke lock, reversed and headed for home. We were immediately locked up again and again a hard turn broke lock. Every time we broke lock, it took about 30 seconds before the Bandits achieved another lock-on. We couldn't relax for a second, and it was a series of gut-wrenching high G turns, as we worked our way south. We knew that if we could keep it up long enough, without taking a missile up the tail pipe, we would eventually run the MiGs out of gas. (Years later, the thought occurs: Why didn't we call in some fighters if there were any airborne in the vicinity. The answer is that we were just too damn busy trying to keep the bandits off our tail, and out of a position from which he could fire effectively into our cone of vulnerability. There was no time to think about anything else).

It got to be a routine which was being played out in intervals of seconds. After the bandits managed to acquire a lock-on, I would yell; "CHAFF" and, as soon as the BN had dumped some chaff, he would yell; "PULL," and I would yank on some heavy Gs in wild turns, mostly diving, sometimes climbing...each time managing to break lock for those precious thirty seconds until finally we were down on the water where it was so black. Every time we broke lock, and after a few turns, we would again try to

gradually work our way south, heading for home.

When you are at max power, it is awfully hard to hold the airplane right down on the water because your experience and the rapid scanning of the instruments keeps telling you that you have to have enough room to maneuver...but every time you get above 500 feet, the bandits achieve lock-on. When you have been on solid instruments in wild turns at 450 knots for a long time and are growing weary, it is easy to lose 300 feet in a hard turn. But if your wing tip catches the crest of a wave, the game is all over. At that speed, it is like hitting a stone wall. To help keep from crashing into the sea, I had rolled in a lot of nose up trim. This required a lot of forward pressure on the stick, but it assured that a slight relaxation on the stick would result in a climb away from the water...a much safer course than allowing an inadvertent descent. It was hard to hold her down and the turns became much more measured and concentration on the flight instruments was intense. Each time we relaxed enough to come up around 500 feet, the warning gear flashed on to show we were about to be locked up. "CHAFF" and "PULL" some more, much more cautiously now below 300 feet AGL to break lock and put out that Red light. Finally, having missed us on that intercept, the bandits broke off the attack. Red Crown reported them heading north, so we climbed to Angels 20 for the return to Danang...low on fuel, with wet flight suits and a very tired right arm. Was that exciting enough for you, Mr. Leach?

In later years I sometimes wondered what it might have been like in the darkened compartment of the ship's CIC. Were sailors watching this drama on their board, or was the information coming from a "College Eye" aircraft on station somewhere watching us. In any event, someone could see us and was watching the whole show, and I wondered if a cheer went up when we finally broke loose. This night in an attack aircraft was sure different from my earlier days in fighters when the aircraft carried offensive armament and a pilot could turn around and engage the enemy. Well, it was a good night's work anyway.

Not all the missions were as exciting as Rolling Thunder or Armed Recon. Many were dull, though effective, like the TPQs which were capable of dropping bombs from altitude, night or day, through a solid undercast, with acceptable accuracy on a concentration of enemy troops. It must have been terribly shocking for the enemy troops bedded down for the night to suddenly feel the concussion of a large drop right on their position.

Of course, the overall favorites of Marine pilots were the close air support (CAS) missions for troops in contact. After the sophistication of a "systems delivery" in RP VI in the black of night, it was a pleasant diversion to go back to "iron gunsight"

An Intruder of VMA (AW)-225 Vagabonds loaded with twenty-two 500 pound bombs enroute to its assigned target during a January 1971 mission over Vietnam. (USMC by GYSGT H.A. Mahan)

Ordnancemen load an A-6A of VMA (AW)-533 for a mission over Vietnam during 1971. It is armed with 500 pound bombs with fuse extenders and Rockeye CBUs indicating that it is being prepared for a close air support (CAS) or other anti-personnel mission. (John Santucci)

daylight attack again. We had some great dive bombers like Bruce Beckman and Gordon Emery. Gordon was a real "Cool Hand Luke," a superb airman, quiet, reserved, a gentleman, but deadly. Flying a two plane section with Gordon against bunkers and gun emplacements on a ridge top, we had to attack perpendicular to the ridge line and over our own troops. If you dropped "long," the bomb fell harmlessly down the far side of the mountain. To drop "short" meant that our ordnance could land among the friendlies who had been trying to climb that ridge and take it from the enemy. It was a great feeling to hear the FAC calling bullseyes and BDA on the enemy bunkers and emplacements, while seeing our troops coming out of their holes and starting up the slope even as we were rolling in on our last run. What trust! What confidence! What expertise! What good luck!

The best CAS missions came as diverts from another assigned mission (this usually meant that troops were in contact and needed help fast). We took off with a full load of 500 pound GP bombs hung on the multiple ejector racks (MERs) and, after switching through the various frequencies and radio nets, were directed to check in with an Air Force FAC flying an O-1, who was working the DMZ area. We got out charts for the new mission, and started looking for the FAC. He read us target data on a heavy caliber artillery site just north of the DMZ which was firing on our troops, keeping them pinned down. The FAC said he would put some smoke on the target. We spotted his second rocket and he gave us aiming instructions from that mark.

That area in the lower part of RP I was defended by some AAA, probably 37MM, and there were heavy machine guns to watch out for as well; MAG 11 had dictated an SOP of one bomb run only in that area. We came in from over the water north of the DMZ and behind the artillery batteries which were pounding the troops in the vicinity of the Rockpile. Although we picked up the smoke marker, we could not see the target, so we rolled in high and slow to have more time to acquire the target visually. The artillery pieces were described as heavy-caliber and positioned west to east along and behind the DMZ. The intervalometer was set to kick off the bombs in pairs in a long string. Only after we started down the chute did we pick up some guns, and they were firing! We had just enough time to adjust the aiming point backwards by going steeper, so that we could start laying the string just before the first gun. Passing through about 7,000 feet, we had a visual on all the guns lined up in a row, five of them, and could adjust our track to walk the gunsight (reticle) right down the row of guns. We pulled out a little low because of having to adjust on the way down, but our twenty-eight bombs

had come off the aircraft in a long string of fourteen pairs impacting right on the guns as they were firing. We pulled out of the run headed for the beach and turned to take a look. Smoke and dust was coming up from a string of detonations along the line of the gun emplacements. I have never heard anyone shout as loud and excited as that FAC, screaming about direct hits on the guns and the great BDA. It sounded like he was going to jump right through our headsets. We looked at each other and grinned in our oxygen masks. THAT will make your day! Fly ten of those in the Marine Corps and they will give you an Air Medal.

There was an air war down South too (south of the DMZ), but it was not much of an air war. It was more of a training area for aircraft going north. My recollections of air work south of the DMZ in 1967 and 1968 was of either light or moderate ground fire by light weapons, or no ground fire at all. Working the Ashau Valley, for example, was not that much more dangerous than dropping on Inky Barley at Yuma. There were no MiGs, no SAMs and no radar-directed guns. The contrast in debriefing was stark. Aircraft returning from Ashau or other local targets reported occasional light fire from small-caliber weapons. But aircraft returning from the upper route packages of North Vietnam reported heavy caliber gunfire, estimated in the hundreds of weapons, in a pattern of well-directed, well-disciplined and, therefore, very accurate fire. The Red River Rats described RP VI as the most heavily defended area in the history of aerial warfare. As a military man, it was great to have been part of that experience, but we lost some very good people, including my own B/N, Steve Kott, and my skipper and good friend, Lou Abrams.

They had some big stuff up there in addition to the 37MM and 57MM guns. Heading home from a raid one night, the sky had turned black again and we were cruise-climbing slowly back to altitude (around 22,000 feet). All was black and quiet except for the red glow of the instruments and the muffled hiss of air over the airframe, when...BAM!! A huge orange airburst way above us...probably 85 or 100MM. They were after somebody up there...glad it wasn't me.

CAS below the DMZ was sometimes a problem because of weather. With an overcast, or a broken layer of clouds, it was hard to find the target, make any kind of a sensible dive on it, or any kind of a sensible pull-out. However, it was not that bad for rockets. If you could work your way under the overcast and find enough room to maneuver in the valleys, you could still fire rockets, especially up into the caves, if you could find them or be directed to them. HVARs were fun. I could never understand why some people short-changed us on HVAR allotments and equipment. The HVAR was a good weapon.

Although the danger in the air war down south was, for the A-6 people, considered minimal compared to the upper route packs, we nevertheless had to tip our hats to the helicopters and

An EA-6A Intruder of VMCJ-1 being refueled at Danang on 30 January 1970. The EA-6A received its combat baptism of fire during November of 1966. VMCJ-1 also operated EF-10Bs, RF-4Bs and RF-8As. (USMC by LCPL G.A. Martinez)

other low and slow types who sometimes had to face heavy machine gun fire and shoulder fired missiles under conditions of prolonged exposure. I would rather be in an A-6.

Except for CAS, as you moved north, the missions became more interesting. "Seeding" missions, for example, were very interesting. A seed was a 500 pound bomb modified with special fusing to act like a mine. It took considerable ability to carefully and accurately lay a pattern of these bombs at a river crossing, at very low altitude, at night. You wanted the seeds in the water at the crossing, so that when a metal object moved close to the mine, it detonated. It was a systems run at night, over the beach to a river point and toward the foothills and mountains for best pattern deployment. And don't forget to pull up or pull a hard turn after the drop or you will pick up some rocks. Although it was safer to run from the other direction, it was too difficult to get down low enough, fast enough to be able to steady out for the B/N in order for him to come up on his aiming point quickly and smoothly enough for a decent drop.

Usually by the time the North Vietnamese heard us in our run, it was too late for them to effectively interfere with our drop. I do remember one night when the ground fire was especially accurate and intense. It was right on us each time we crossed the beach, and we were taking a lot of fire! How come they can see us so well? They must have the first-string gunners working tonight! The answer came on the next run, when we passed through a wisp of cloud that reflected the light on the ship. During an IFR take-off, the nose wheel landing light had been used to pick up the runway centerline during the takeoff roll. In the busy exchanges of radio dialogue and changes of frequencies after lift-off, the light pivoted from forward to straight down as the nose gear retracted. So now we had a beacon shining straight down for the gunners to aim at! The moral of the story: Don't give them an aiming point to shoot at!

After having planted seeds at strategic points for several nights, each night having to make numerous runs because the seeded area was very restricted, it was disheartening to hear a "Yellowbird" on the frequency as we headed north one night. He was attacking the bed of the river at the point we had just seeded. In his ignorance he kept up an ecstatic running report of numerous secondary explosions as he unwittingly detonated all of our carefully planted seeds. Something was truly wrong with his mission assignment or control.

Napalm and snakeye deliveries were also fun because they were low level daylight missions which we did not get too often. Hunter-killer missions were high and effective. These were two aircraft missions which were developed in VMA (AW)-242 in order to reduce the effectiveness of enemy radar. We needed to do something about the enemy search radar, which tracked us on the way north, and the enemy fire-control radar, which helped direct the SAMs and AAA, so the paired attack mission was developed. In a section launch, the strike aircraft was an A-6A

armed with Shrike radar-homing missiles. The second aircraft was an EA-6A from VMCJ-1. When the EA-6A picked up the enemy radar emissions, it transmitted azimuth information to the A-6 which then pulled slightly ahead and fired it's Shrike. The red cockpit warning light would continue to blink for a while as the radar made it's sweeps, but then the light would go off in about ninety seconds or so, depending upon the distance from the target when we fired the Shrike. It was a nice mission while it lasted. The enemy soon caught on to the mission, especially if they could pick out the blips of two aircraft. They then would sweep for only short intervals, changing from one site to another for a few sweeps from another direction, but would not stay up long enough for us to get a shot at them. This mission was later modified for other aircraft, using other systems, tactics, and weapons.

It was sometimes wildly exciting in the execution of the mission, if you were not too busy just staying alive, and even years later when you gave it some thought, your pulse would quicken. I could never understand how the BNs could take such wild gyrations without barfing all over the cockpit. When you are taking fire and jinking madly just to stay out of it, the BN, with his head in the boot (the hood over his radar scope), being tossed up, down, and sideways, must have been on the verge of vomiting, yet none ever got sick during that intense reaction time between leaving the IP and completion of egress when the bird started back down the eastern or western track and a climb to altitude.

Picking up from the valley floor one night to clear Thud Ridge, then sliding down the other side, we were scooting along about 800 feet AGL when there in front of us appeared what looked like a North Vietnamese barracks, all lit up. No time to stare...we immediately began taking heavy ground fire. We were north of Hanoi and heading east towards the water. I keyed the mike to the BN and said; "Hey, Rudy (Schwanda), pull your head out of the boot and take a look at this!" Rudy, a short, rugged BN and a pleasure to fly with, drew his head back up out the hood and took a quick look around. The flashes of orange and white airbursts through the canopy lit up his face. He took one look at all the tracers and exploding flak following our airplane and hollered, "GODDAM! LET'S GET THE F..K OUTA-HERE!!" Wise counsel, Rudy. Wise Counsel.

You cannot talk North without mention of the "black boxes" that kept the fire just far enough off the bird to keep the airbursts from making holes. Anyone who went deep without his black boxes in good working order was not too smart. Unsung heroes, of course, were the VMCJ-1 crews who did a lot of sophisticated things, especially ECM and Photo-Recon. They could bring back next day photography that would show the "footprint" of your drop, but were most dearly loved for their ability to jam enemy fire control systems, throwing their switches at just the right time. One night, while running in over Vinh from the sea and after giving the code word passing the IP in the attack, I heard the friendly voice of a VMCJ-1 "gunner" (Warrant Officer) working the ECM panel of an EA-6A. He came on the frequency saying, "Better get out of there, Skipper, they're hosing you down." Taking my eyes from the scan of the steering symbology on the scope and my flight instruments, I glanced up at the mirrors for just a second. There was the most beautiful display of white airbursts forming a curving string from where we had rolled out of our turn in from IP on the attack run. The AAA was truly like a stream from a fire hose. Those were not drops of water! In a couple of seconds we were clean and out of there, but it was a good feeling knowing that VMCJ was out there over the water zapping those fire control systems which were directing the guns against us in our run.

The A-6 people were lucky to have education and instruction coming from such capable and experienced crewmen as Ken Bateman for the pilots, and Dave Villeneuve and Nellie Dye for the BNs. Also there was Gordon Emery whom we loaned from 242 Operations to the Air Force, when they brought the F-

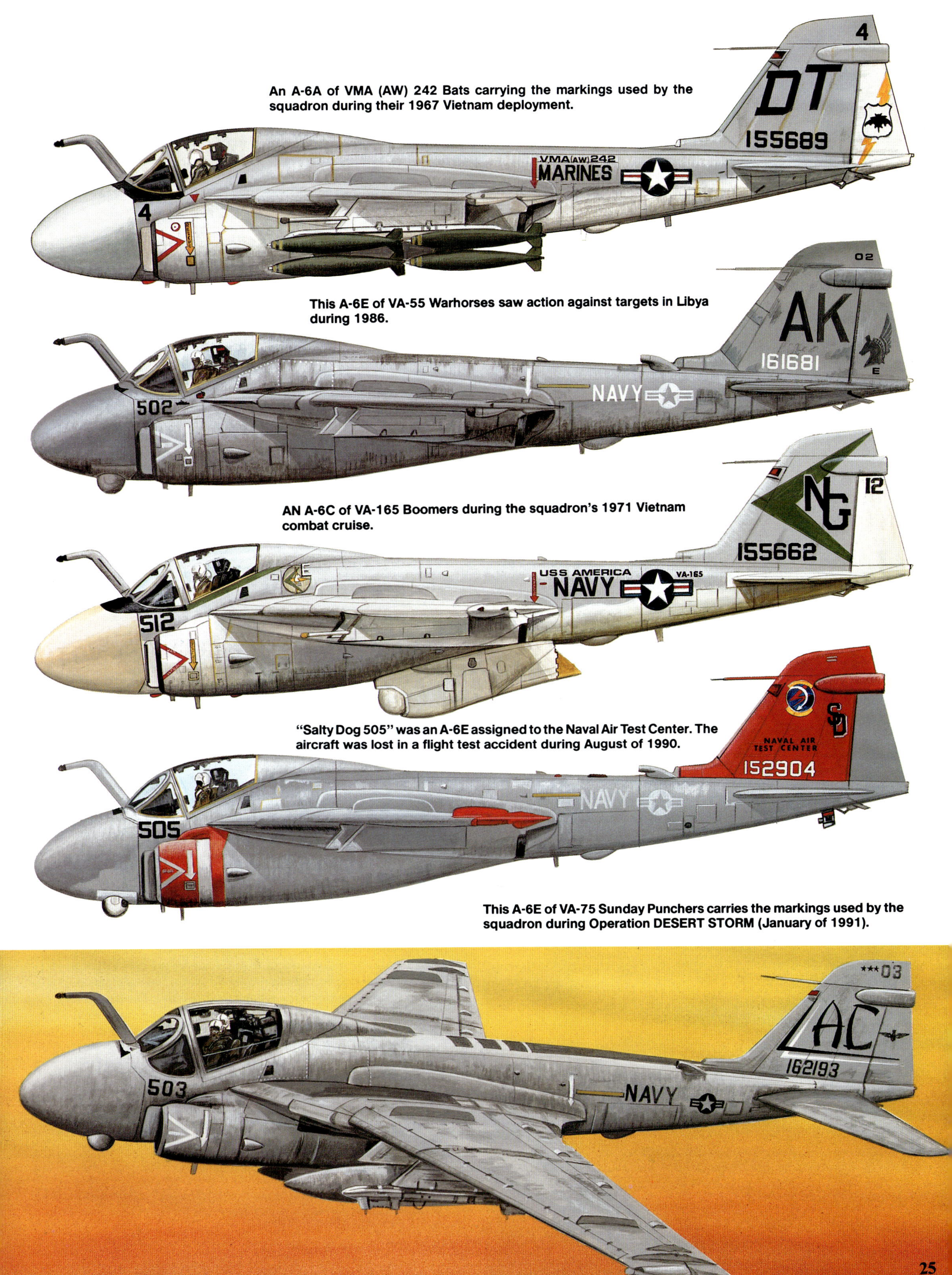

An A-6A of VMA (AW) 242 Bats carrying the markings used by the squadron during their 1967 Vietnam deployment.

This A-6E of VA-55 Warhorses saw action against targets in Libya during 1986.

AN A-6C of VA-165 Boomers during the squadron's 1971 Vietnam combat cruise.

"Salty Dog 505" was an A-6E assigned to the Naval Air Test Center. The aircraft was lost in a flight test accident during August of 1990.

This A-6E of VA-75 Sunday Punchers carries the markings used by the squadron during Operation DESERT STORM (January of 1991).

111s in-country. Gordon was sent to talk to them about terrain clearance and the low-level attack mission (which the A-6 had been flying). The F-111 drivers were apparently not paying full attention because they promptly flew two aircraft into the sides of hills and then grounded the aircraft.

The A-6 also mounted a camera at the B/N's station so that he could take pictures of the presentations he observed during the attack. This Radar Scope Photography (RSP) was displayed in the Ready Room for each major target. It enabled BNs and pilots unfamiliar with a particular target to view and study pictures of the IP's and targets as they would appear on the scope during the attack run. You could see it all before you actually struck the target.

The isolated Special Forces camps also had a friend in the A-6 because it could see in the dark and in rotten weather. When these camps were under attack in bad weather and were unable to call in visual strikes for support, they could still call in an A-6 strike around their position. To make this mission feasible, A-6 people like Marty Egan went to Special Forces camps to set up radar reflectors in trees and elsewhere. The radar returns form these reflectors enable the BNs to calculate and set up a systems run for dropping bombs in foul weather when no other support was available.

An aggravating circumstance occurred in targeting with disquieting frequency. Sometimes the A-6 missions going north would be scheduled with identical and repetitive target data. The second time I hit Hoa Lac, for example, my ordnance load, my TOT (time on target), my code word, etc., were all identical to those of a mission a few nights earlier. This was almost a setup for gunners on the ground. They could set their watches by it and it was dangerous for the aircrews. I was so burned up at being set up, and after having had a hosing down the first time over Hoa Lac, that I released at 5,000 feet instead of the usual 1,800 feet AGL. The difference in ground-fire reaction is oftentimes different, depending on altitude of drop and other factors. In this instance, it so happened that the first attack on Hoa Lac drew tremendously heavy fire, whereas the attack a few nights later drew no appreciable reaction. This same circumstance of identical, repetitive targeting occurred down at Vinh a couple of times, and elsewhere. Sometimes the aircraft drew a worse reaction and sometimes a lesser reaction. It was not something you could plan for. Generally, however, the A-6 crews recognized an increased danger in identical, repetitive targeting in that it served to prime the enemy for the oncoming attack.

Someone was always watching. There were lots of eyes in that black, night sky, some friendly, some not so friendly. It was both good and bad depending on who was looking at you and when. Air Intelligence could tell if you made it to your target. They watched the night Lou Abrams got flipped over by a missile on his attack run, recovered low and still went back in to deliver with pin-point accuracy. The next morning Lou was awakened and called up to the Wing General's office. 7th Air Force in Saigon already had photography of the bomb damage and had sent a congratulatory message after the Photo-Recon people had confirmed the "footprint" of the drop from Lou's air-craft, about as near perfect a drop as you can get under conditions which were about as bad as you can get.

Those night-sky scanners could also tell if you did not make it to your target or maybe why you did not make it home that night. They saw where Val Bacik got it north of Haiphong near the Chinese border. When Abrams went down going into Haiphong, Air Intelligence could point to where he was hit, where his blip went off the scope as he was crossing the beach. I hope they were watching too when Gordon Emery and I took a two-plane section up to Haiphong on a search for wreckage or any other signs in the unlikely event that the crew had been able to punch out over the water. But it is hard to search at low altitude when you have to be so alert for enemy activity and also keep the other aircraft in sight. Searching higher gave better visibility, but greater exposure. There seemed to be nothing else up there that day to draw fire except maybe us, but we did not press our luck and stayed feet wet.

Out of this deployment came an abiding respect for enemy fire-discipline. As I said before, the enemy gunners were good, but they did not waste any ammunition, probably because they had to carry a good part of it on their backs and probably because it was not that easy to get. If the target was not worth defending that night (maybe they had moved their supplies), they might not shoot. It was possible to hit the same target three different times and get three different reactions depending upon whether the enemy might have been short of ammunition that night, might not have needed much protection that night or might not have wanted to reach up high for you. On the other hand, some nights you might get a violent reaction from the same target. The reaction depended on a lot of factors. On an AR, for example, when you know the bad guys are down there at particular coordinates, but there is no reaction to light up their exact position or otherwise reveal their pin-point location, we could play our little game. We would make a systems run dropping only one bomb about every five minutes or so, dropping sometimes on one suspected spot, say on one bank of a river crossing, and sometimes moving to another suspected spot nearby, say another point of a river bank staging area. After two or three of these drops, we had stirred up the hornet's nest. Sometimes to further provoke them and give them a false aiming point, we would flick on a landing light for a second (if the night were VFR) and then change direction and altitude. Then, when the AAA batteries opened up on us showing us their exact position, we would come in from a different direction and drop the whole load right on them. Don't you know that they were mad as hell! We often had the option of making a systems run at altitude, maybe because of terrain, or visually dive bombing, whatever appeared most effective at the time. Again, better to hit them up there than to take rockets down at Danang a few days later.

Would I do anything differently if I could do it all over again? You bet. I would find more time for the troops and more occasions for Meritorious Mast for the men whose efforts and devotion to duty were most often overlooked or whose recognition was neglected in the busy workday of the combat environment. I have in mind, for example, taxiing into the fuel pits one night around midnight, shutting down my radio while taking on fuel (and therefore "deaf" to radio warnings), both engines turning up to supply electrical power for the fuel transfer system, and so was unable to hear other noises, like sirens. There came a banging on the canopy, and as it opened, a ground crewman was pulling my helmet away from my head and shouting in my ear, "INCOMING! INCOMING!...SHUT HER DOWN AND MOVE OUT!!!" As I scrambled down the side of the aircraft, the man grabbed me and pulled me through the (now) darkness of the revetment area to where we finally tumbled down into a bunker where someone eventually got a candle lit. Then came a couple of hits nearby, though not on our flight line. I never did get to properly thank that troop who had left the protection of his bunker to help the man refueling me and to drag me through the darkness out of harm's way. This I have always regretted and been saddened by. Would I give him a big hug if I could see him again today? You bet I would.

Wings folded and tied down, an A-6A of VMA (AW)-332 Polka Dots rests on the ramp at MCAS Cherry Point, N.C., on 17 May 1969. The engine air intake covers are Red. (USMC by Jim Sullivan)

LTC Larry P. Beasley, USAF (Ret)

...had one of the most varied and interesting military aviation careers of the dozens of military aviators I have interviewed in twenty-five years of writing on military aviation.

Larry was born in Marion, Indiana, on 11 February 1935. Upon graduation from high school in Crete, Illinois, he enlisted in the Marine Corps on 9 June 1953. After boot camp and specialty training he was assigned to VMJ-1 at K-3, Pohang AB, Korea. In January of 1955, he was selected to attend Naval Aviation Cadet Training at NAS Pensacola, Florida. Upon graduation from flight school in September of 1956, he was commissioned a Second Lieutenant in the Marine Corps and assigned to VMF-333 at MCAS Miami, Florida. While there he flew the AD-6 and the FJ-3 Fury. In July of 1958, he was reassigned to the 2nd Air Naval Gunfire Liaison Company at Camp Lejuene, as a FAC and later shipped out to the Mediterranean Sea to serve in Beirut, Lebanon, in the Summer of 1958.

In June of 1959, he was discharged from the Marine Corps and entered Miami University at Oxford, Ohio. In 1960, he transferred from the Marine Corps Reserve to the 162nd TFS of the Ohio ANG, at Springfield, Ohio, where he flew F-84Fs. During October of 1961, during the Berlin Crisis, he was recalled to active duty and sent to the 166th TFS of the Ohio ANG, which was based at Etain AB, France.

In July of 1962, COL Beasley was selected for Career Reserve Status and assigned to the 45th TFS at MacDill AFB, Florida. After his completion of Jump School at Fort Benning, Georgia, he was reassigned to the 47th TFS and served in this squadron as the squadron weapons officer until 1964 when he was reassigned to the 555th TFS, the first USAF operational F-4 Phantom squadron. While at MacDill, COL Beasley finished his studies at the University of Tampa and received his degree during 1965 and was selected for Regular Air Force status. In November of 1964, the 555th TFS deployed to Naha AB, Okinawa, and in April 1965, COL Beasley volunteered for TDY at Bien Hoa AB, RVN. While on TDY, he flew over seventy combat missions with the 1st Air Commando Squadron in the A-1E and O-1F.

Upon his return to the 555th the squadron was transferred to PACAF, first serving at Naha from November of 1965, to February of 1966, when it was reassigned to the 8th TFW at Ubon RTAB, Thailand. Upon completion of his combat tour, he was reassigned to the 4455th CCTS, Davis Monthan AFB, Arizona, as an F-4 IP. In October of 1968, he was selected to be the first Air Force exchange pilot to fly the A-6 Intruder. He went to VA-128 for training at NAS Whidbey Island, Washington, completing his training in July of 1969. He was assigned to VA-165 and deployed aboard USS AMERICA during April of 1970, headed for the Gulf of Tonkin. These are some of his recollections of that cruise.

Air Force MAJ Doyle Balentine preflights the weapons load on his A-6A of VA-165. The squadron was deployed aboard USS AMERICA during September of 1970. (USAF)

MAJ Doyle Balentine (left) and MAJ Larry Beasley were the first USAF exchange crew to fly the A-6 in combat. They were attached to VA-165 operating off USS AMERICA. (U.S. Navy via Beasley)

When the F-111s went into combat during 1968, they experienced a high loss rate. The Air Force wanted to compare what they had been doing with the F-111 to what the Navy was doing with the A-6, so they picked a crew for exchange duty with the Navy. I was the pilot and Doyle Ballantine was the navigator. We were supposed to operate as a crew, but the Navy did not want to pair up a couple of Air Force guys who were brand-new carrier pilots in one of their airplanes, so we got split up when we got to our squadron, VA-165 Boomers.

VA-165 was an unusual squadron, in that they operated A-6As, A-6Bs and A-6Cs. We were deployed aboard USS AMERICA (CV-66) and the scariest part of the whole cruise for me was not the combat...it was operating off the boat! The A-6C posed some particular problems, especially at night. The large sensor pod on the centerline created a great deal of drag and if you loaded up with twenty-two Mk 82 bombs, it was the same as having an extra twenty-eight bombs in drag when you added that sensor. On dark, wet nights, it was always a little bit of an adventure to get it off the deck.

The A-6 was a super airplane. The bombing system, when it was peaked, was able to lay the bombs right in there. One of the most outstanding things about the airplane, in my opinion, was flying with the ADI. I could go down to the range at night and fly a dozen loft-bombing profiles, on instruments, and get CEPs like I never saw with anything in the Air Force. But the emphasis should be placed on the Intruder's use as an all-weather attacker. It was not that great a dive bomber, even compared with the F-4, and I never thought it should be operated in a flight of four, for instance. If you flew it in the all weather attack mission, it was the best airplane over there for that...better than the F-111. Of course, as fighter pilot, I always felt kind of naked without any

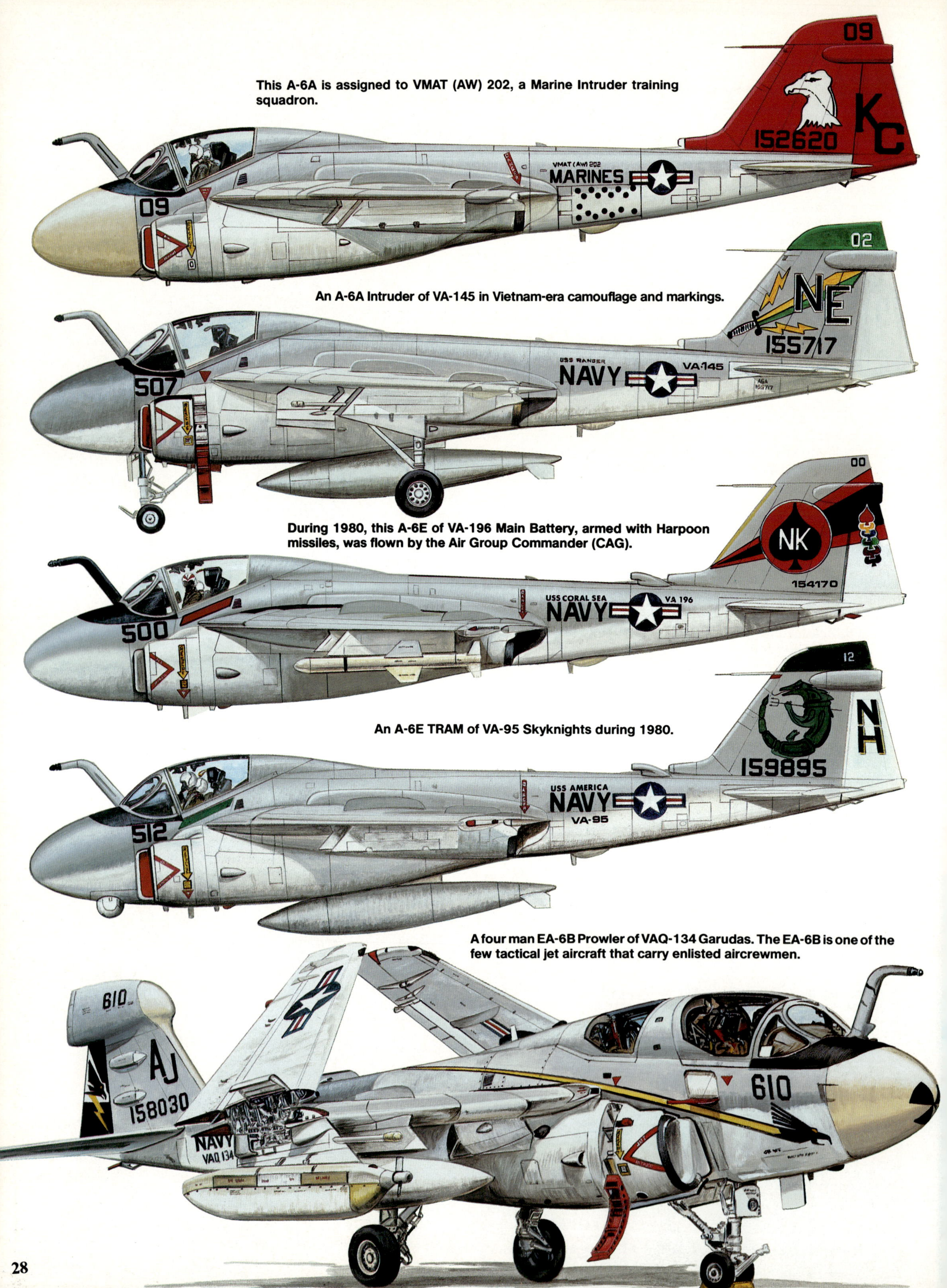

This A-6A is assigned to VMAT (AW) 202, a Marine Intruder training squadron.

An A-6A Intruder of VA-145 in Vietnam-era camouflage and markings.

During 1980, this A-6E of VA-196 Main Battery, armed with Harpoon missiles, was flown by the Air Group Commander (CAG).

An A-6E TRAM of VA-95 Skyknights during 1980.

A four man EA-6B Prowler of VAQ-134 Garudas. The EA-6B is one of the few tactical jet aircraft that carry enlisted aircrewmen.

An A-6A Intruder is positioned on the carrier deck.

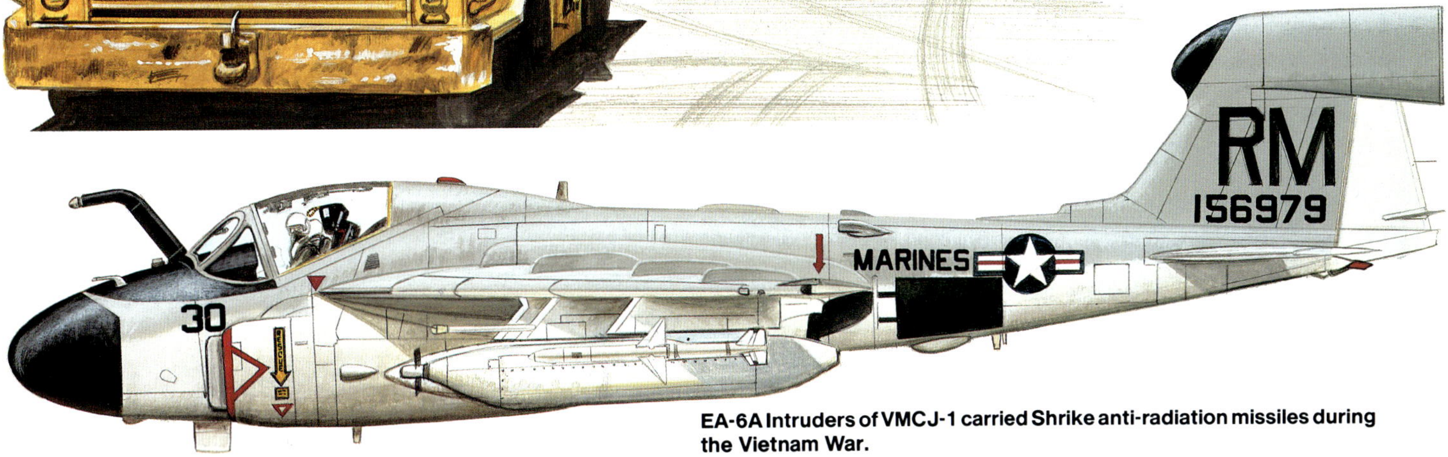

EA-6A Intruders of VMCJ-1 carried Shrike anti-radiation missiles during the Vietnam War.

This A-6E of VA-35 Black Panthers is armed with Mk-20 Rockeye bombs and Shrike missiles.

MAJ Larry Beasley dismounts after a bombing mission over North Vietnam. The built-in crew boarding ladder on the A-6 allowed for easy access to the cockpit. (USAF)

forward-firing armament. If I had ever gotten mixed up with MiGs, I wouldn't have had any way to defend myself.

The A-6C was an experimental airplane, which they started working on during 1969. Grumman had added a large sensor pod to the centerline of the airplane. This pod contained low light level television and infrared sensors which were slaved to the radar. The idea was to be able to visually identify targets which you picked up on your radar. It was the forerunner of the A-6E TRAM of today. We were tasked with combat evaluation of the system. I got the first aircraft from the factory on 25 February 1970, and we deployed to Southeast Asia on 6 April. That gave us less than a month to get pilots and maintenance people qualified to fly and maintain the aircraft. Something like that would never have been done in the Air Force. We did the combat evaluation at the same time as the Operational Test and Evaluation (OT&E)! The system worked very well, considering that it was a prototype. It worked much better when we were training in Washington than it did when we got to combat in Vietnam. We thought that the IR was being degraded by the weather, but we later discovered that the equipment was reaching the end of its service life just when we were peaking in the combat evaluation.

The A-6B was optimized for the Wild Weasel or Iron Hand mission. There were only nineteen A-6Bs (converted from A-6As) and I think we had six or eight of them in the squadron. Doyle Balentine was the squadron's project officer for the Standard Arm missile, which was the primary Iron Hand weapon. That meant that the two big squadron projects were being run by Air Force officers!

Most of the targets we bombed during this period were on the Ho Chi Minh Trail, since the bombing moratorium on most of North Vietnam which went into effect in March of 1968 deprived us of a lot of the more significant targets. I got fifty-five combat missions before my tour was up, and about thirty of them were night missions. The weather seemed to alternate. If it was good over the Gulf of Tonkin, it was bad over land, and if it was bad in the Gulf, it was good over land. There were a lot of times when we made night bombing runs in the soup and never saw the ground. The only indications we had that it was combat was the flash of the bombs lighting up the undercast. Coming back to the boat at night was still the most exciting part of all of these missions! The biggest enemy of the carrier pilot is vertigo. As far as just flying the airplane on instruments was concerned, it was never a problem for me...but on those dark, moonless nights, when it was as dark as the inside of an ink bottle, and there was absolutely no horizon, you could get into trouble. As I flew the approach, and when I transferred from the gauges to the carrier optical landing system...the ball...I sometimes would get a raging case of vertigo which I fought all the way down to the deck. If you were unlucky enough to get a bolter, you were right back out there again, forced to go through the same ordeal. I have the highest admiration for the Navy crews that do this for a living!

Larry completed his exchange tour in October of 1970 and was assigned to the 57th Fighter Weapons Wing at Nellis AFB, Nevada. His duties during this tour were as the 57th FWW Weapons Officer. In November of 1972, he was selected to introduce the F-4E slatted-wing TISEO aircraft to Southeast Asia. He deployed with the first contingent in November of 1972, to Udorn RTAB and was assigned to the 555th TFS. The TISEO system was similar to that pioneered in the A-6C. While at Udorn, Larry flew in Linebacker II and served in the capacities of Flight Commander, Assistant Operations Officer and, in May of 1973, as the Chief of Weapons and Tactics for the 432nd TRW. In October of 1973, he was reassigned to the Tactical Air Warfare Center at Eglin AFB, Florida, where he served as Chief of the Air-to-Air Missile Test Branch, responsible for testing AIM-9J, AIM-9L, AIM-7E and AIM-7F missiles.

Larry Beasley retired as a LTC after suffering a heart attack during 1976. His association with the A-6 led to a job with Grumman. He represents Grumman at Nellis AFB, Nevada.

The crew of this A-6A of VA-65 Tigers is directed to a parking spot on the flight deck of USS INDEPENDENCE after a 1971 mission. The squadron designator was painted on the drop tanks in Black. (U.S. Navy)

The band around the rear fuselage identifies this Intruder to be a KA-6D of VA-165 off USS CONSTELLATION, during July of 1971. The first flight of the KA-6D tanker was 23 May 1966 and a total of seventy-eight A-6A/Es were modified to the KA-6D configuration. (U.S. Navy)

Mike Schuster

...got his Navy Wings of Gold in February of 1968. He remained in the Training Command as an instructor for an additional fourteen months before reporting to VA-42, the A-6 RAG, in June of 1969. Upon completion of the A-6 pilot training program in VA-42, he was assigned to VA-75, under the command of CDR Deke Bordone. He made two Med Deployments before reassignment to VA-42 as an instructor pilot. In the meantime, VA-75 had deployed to WESTPAC embarked in USS SARATOGA to participate in the 1972 Linebacker bombing campaign against North Vietnam. Mike picks up the story at that point:

After three months on the line, VA-75 had lost a couple of aircraft, including one flown by Don Linland with my former BN, Roger Lerseth, aboard. MATWING asked for volunteers to replace the lost crews. I volunteered to rejoin the squadron and BN Don Sekowski, who had been in the A-6 community for a while, but never in VA-75, joined me. That was in August of 1972, and the deployment ended in February of 1973.

My most memorable mission occurred on the night of 20 December 1972. My BN was Jerry Mullins, AKA "Moon" (everyone in the Navy who is named Mullins is automatically nicknamed "Moon"). We had been in the squadron together on my previous deployment, so they crewed us up again when I rejoined the squadron. We were familiar with each other's habits and idiosyncrasies and we were comfortable together.

This was a typical night mission. What we would do is launch four A-6s, which would then go in single-ship, either sequentially on the same target, or on different targets. The aircraft in front of us was flown by Ken Knapp and John Fuller and, when they came out, they told us that there was lot of AAA and SAM activity. Our target was a truck park near Haiphong Harbor. The North Vietnamese were off-loading Chinese Communist ships onto these trucks, and since we were prohibited from bombing the ships, we had to wait and go after the trucks.

We used Red Crown, the Navy ship which provided command and control and radar advisories to aircraft flying over the North, as our final navigation fix before running into the target at 200 feet. We were dropping 500 pound Snakeye bombs. We went in low level, and then popped up to 300 to 400 feet to drop the bombs. We started getting a lot of AAA fire and took a couple of light hits in the bottom of the starboard wing. As we pulled off the target, Jerry noted that they had shot a couple of SAMs at us. We were so low that the SAM radar could not track us, but they were manually guiding them. We were under a fairly low and thin overcast, so we could see the flame from the rocket motors as the North Vietnamese tried to guide them. This was a typical tactic, and if they could get the SAM close enough to us, they would manually detonate the warhead.

Jerry was preoccupied with watching these SAMs and I was occupied with flying the airplane and with watching AAA streaks and flashes all around us, so neither of was watching the terrain avoidance radar. There was slight break in the overcast, and just about the time we got to that, we took a hit from a 23MM gun right in the refueling probe. There was a full moon that night, so it was pretty bright on top of the overcast and down low where there were breaks in the overcast. When the refueling probe got hit, I looked up and saw, by the light of the moon, a karst ridge right in front of us! It looked like a collision with the ground was imminent, so I yanked on the stick as hard as I could. We cleared most of the ridge...but not everything on it.

We ran through a couple of trees, doing considerable damage to both wings and fuselage. We zoomed to what was really not a safe altitude for that area, and once we had determined that the airplane was still flyable, Jerry cautioned me that we were really too high, and urged me to get back down on the deck until we could get feet wet and back out of the SAM envelope. The two SAMs that had so distracted us that we almost ran into the side of a ridge had long since ceased to be a threat, but we knew there were more where they came from.

Once we were clear of North Vietnam, we climbed to altitude and were joined by Dick Engel and Hal King, who looked us over. After noting all the airframe damage, he recommended a no flap, no slat landing on the carrier. We jettisoned all of our external stores, including the multiple ejector bomb racks. We had lost all of our wing fuel as a result of the punctures caused by trees, but with full mains, gas was not a real concern. Unfortunately, we had also lost one of two main hydraulic systems. On the way

An A-6A (BuNo 155628) of VA-115 Arabs off USS MIDWAY on the ramp at Misawa Air Base, Japan, on 20 October 1974. VA-115 made combat cruises aboard MIDWAY during 1971 and 1972, participating in the Linebacker campaign against North Vietnam. (Norman E. Taylor)

This Intruder is assigned to VMA (AW) 332 Polkadots.

A KA-6D Intruder tanker of VA-196 crosses the ramp of USS CORAL SEA.

This A-6E of VA-85 is credited with two Libyan missile boat kills during 1986. The Intruder is armed with AGM-84 Harpoons and AIM-9 Sidewinder missiles.

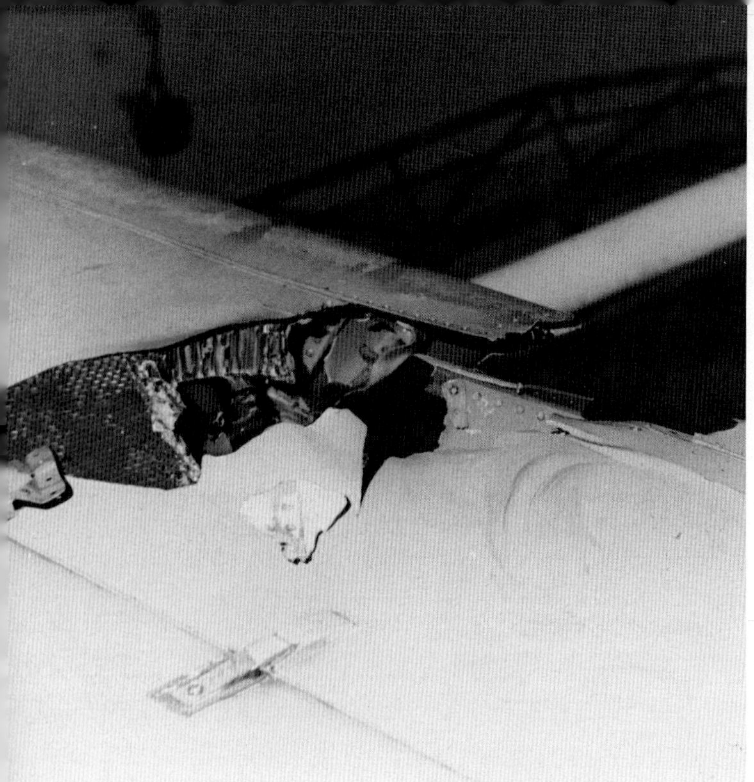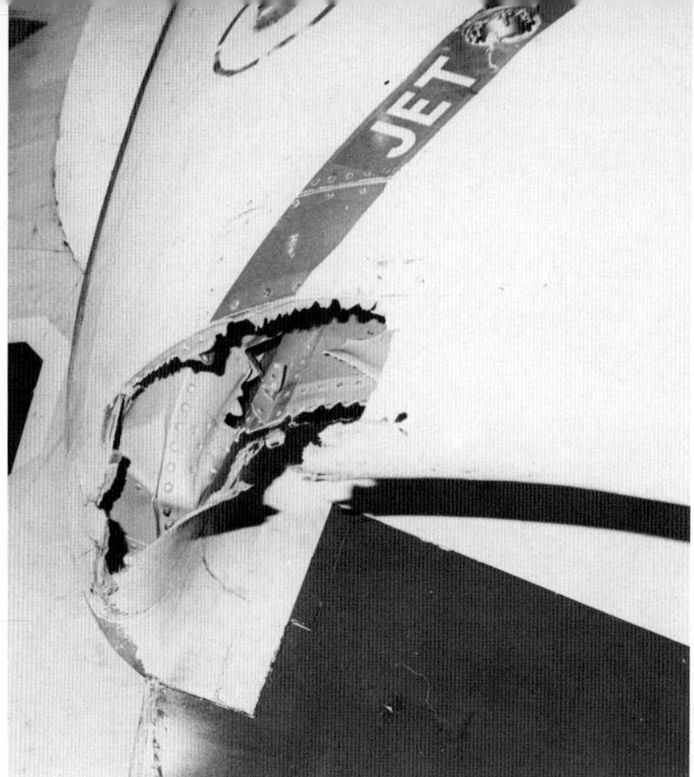

The damage done to the Intruder by the trees was extensive. As a result, the aircraft was parked on the hangar bay and became a source of spare parts for other A-6s within the squadron. (U.S. Navy)

back to the ship, we tried slow-flighting the airplane, to see how fast we would be going when we came aboard. Turned out that the slowest we could fly without flaps and slats was about 22 knots above the maximum engaging speed. The Air Boss got together with the skipper of the ship and they decided to try to bring us aboard. They moved all the airplanes forward and cleared the deck of all personnel except the LSOs. The main concern was that the higher landing speed would overtax an arresting cable, and it would break and whip across the deck, cutting down anyone or anything in it's path.

We came aboard, and it turned out to be a fairly normal approach and landing, except for the fact that my forward vision was obscured by tree sap and leaf stains on the windscreen. We caught the number one wire, my favorite (the LSO used to give me a fair amount of grief about that, but I figured; "Why waste three good wires?") We taxied forward, shut down and the air-plane was taken below and stuck in a corner of the hangar bay, where it remained for the rest of the cruise. It reeked of pine trees, which was a welcome seasonal touch much appreciated by the troops since it was near Christmas. The damage to the airplane was so severe that it was later struck from the inventory. You have probably heard of the "Grumman Iron Works." Well, this was a great example of how Grumman builds tough aircraft!

Mike retired from the Navy in June of 1986, after twenty years of service, which included 2,400 hours in the Intruder. When I interviewed him in January of 1991, he was a First Officer with American Airlines, flying the MD-80. He remembered his A-6 service fondly, stating that he thought there was a lot more camaraderie among the entire A-6 community, as compared to some other communities. Because of the close coordination necessary between the pilot and BN to accomplish the mission, there is more of a sense of teamwork.

An A-6A Intruder of VA-145 Swordsmen off USS RANGER. VA-145 made combat cruises aboard USS ENTERPRISE (1969) and USS RANGER (1970-71 and 1972-73). The Extendable Equipment Platform is swung open from the underside of the fuselage. (Norman E. Taylor)

CAPT Craig "Gator" Chewning

...acquired his nickname on his first deployment. While visiting Barcelona, Spain, with a shipmate, he demonstrated his Cajun background (and both amazed and disgusted his squeamish friend) by eating the head of a crawfish which had been served in a bowl of bouilabaisse.

He had graduated from LSU, then went on to Aviation Officer Candidate School (AOCS) at Pensacola. In his own words, "After they had shaved my head and allowed Marines to beat on me for a week, they informed me that I had 20-25 vision in one eye and I could go home." (20-20 in both eyes is required for military pilots.) When he protested, they explained that he had the option to become a Naval Flight Officer (NFO). They further explained that that would give him the opportunity to ride in high performance aircraft, even if he couldn't fly them. At the time, that meant the A-5 Vigilante, A-3 Skywarrior, F-4 Phantom, E-1s, E-2s or the A-6. Again, according to Chewning, "The only one that I saw in the bunch in which the NFO seemed to have equal responsibility for completion of the mission was the A-6." He completed AOCS with class standing that allowed him his first choice of aircraft and he opted for the Intruder.

After graduation from the training squadron (VA-42) in May of 1971, he deployed to the Mediterranean aboard USS AMERICA with VA-35. He returned from that deployment in December and redeployed to Vietnam with VA-35 in June of 1972, and did not return until April of 1973. VA-35 won the battle E and S safety award on that cruise, losing just two aircraft and one crew in several months of combat. This was followed by two years as an instructor with VA-42. The next two years were spent as ships company aboard USS NIMITZ as Air Traffic Control Officer for two Mediterranean cruises. What flying he did during that time was also done with VA-35.

During 1978, he was reassigned to MATWING ONE at Oceana as NATOPS Model Manager for five different versions of the A-6 (A-6E, A-6B, A-6E CAWS, A-6E TRAM, KA-6D). During 1981 he went to VA-65, aboard USS Eisenhower for one North Atlantic and two Mediterranean cruises. His next assignment was to the staff of Naval Air Forces Atlantic as A-6 Training Officer. In May of 1985, he was assigned to VA-55 as Executive Officer, and one year later took over as CO of VA-55. During this period, he made two Med cruises aboard USS CORAL SEA He was relieved in December of 1987, and reassigned to USS KENNEDY as Operations Officer, a post he held until February of 1989. He returned to Naval Air Forces Atlantic Staff, again as A-6 Training Officer, until reassignment as Commander of Medium Attack Wing One, NAS Oceana in February of 1990. His A-6 career included ten deployments, 1,015 arrested landings and 4,000 hours in the A-6. In all but two years of his career he has been in operational positions. As he contemplated his retirement, Gator said, "This is the only job in the world where you don't have to grow up or say you are sorry for a damn thing!" He loved flying and is proud of the fact that he was able to fly for all but two years of his career.

The nose gear of this VA-52 Knightriders KA-6D Intruder collapsed upon landing aboard USS KITTY HAWK. The flight deck crane was used to raise the nose so that squadron maintenance personnel could lower the nose gear. (Nick Waters)

His perspective on the A-6 spans over two-thirds of the Intruder's career. His recollections of that career follow:

I had 149 combat missions in Vietnam, including multiple missions up North in Route Package 6 and 6B. The most spectacular of these were the Linebacker II missions that we flew at Christmas-time during 1972, which resulted in the POWs coming home. Alpha Strikes, which involved the whole air wing, were usually flown in the Summer and Fall. When the weather got bad in the Winter, everyone stayed home except the A-6s. We would fly at night, in the weather, single ship. Beginning on 18 December, we would launch six A-6s on every-other cycle from each ship. They would form up in two three ship Vees, one at 10,000 feet and one at 11,000 feet. The two Vees would take a pre-determined interval, then head for the North Vietnamese coast. As they got close to the coast, they would begin to let down to coast-in altitude and attack airspeed. Just prior to crossing the coast, they would split. The guy on the left would turn left about 45 degrees to his attack heading, the guy on the right would turn right, and the leader would continue (more or less) straight ahead. Routes across the ground were planned to make sure that no one ran into each other, because when you crossed the coast, all the lights went off. We also had "hard" times on target, which meant that if you were supposed to bomb at 2300, you bombed at 2300. The biggest reason for this was that most of our missions at this time were SAM suppression missions for the B-52 strikes which devastated Hanoi. The B-52s flew in the optimum SAM performance envelope, and they flew straight and level, relying on their own ECM and our effectiveness as SAM killers to ensure their survival. Our normal load was sixteen Rockeye CBUs.

An A-6E of VA-145, which made three combat cruises to Southeast Asia, carries the buddy refueling store on the centerline station. The buddy store allows any Navy aircraft to act as a tanker. (Shinichi Ohtaki)

CAPT W.C. "Gator" Chewning straps into the cockpit of an Intruder assigned to VA-42 at NAS Oceana, Virginia during February of 1991. The aircraft carries low visibility numbers and rescue markings in shades of Gray. (U.S. Navy)

Nineteen of the first batch of A-6As were converted to A-6B standards specifically to perform the Iron Hand anti-SAM mission in Vietnam. The prototype was tested with dummy Standard ARM missiles and a centerline ECM pod. (Grumman)

A KA-6D of VA-55 Warhorses aboard USS CORAL SEA in the Mediterranean during the Spring of 1986. During this deployment, VA-55 participated in attacks on Libyan targets in response to Libyan terrorist attacks. (U.S. Navy)

VMA (AW) 224 made a WESTPAC combat cruise aboard USS CORAL SEA from November of 1971 to July of 1972. They were the first Marine A-6 squadron to fly combat missions from carriers, helping to blunt the North Vietnamese Easter invasion of South Vietnam. (via Nick Waters)

The prototype A-6C carried a sensor pod under the centerline. The success of these tests led to the current A-6E TRAM. (Grumman)

These Blue tailed A-6s are assigned to VMA (AW) 224 Bengals. The Marine Intruders carry the Orange and White Bengals squadron patch on the rudder. (Grumman)

This rewinged A-6E conducted ordnance certification tests which included a wide variety of weapons. The weapons being released here are 2,500 pound simulated mines. (U.S. Navy)

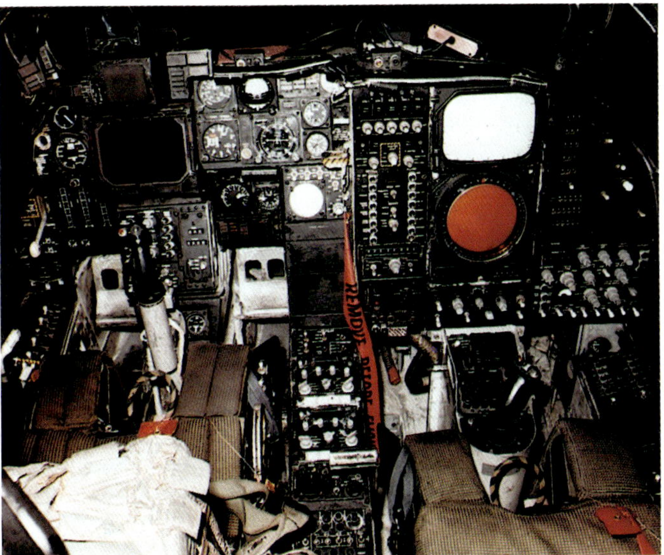

The cockpit of an A-6E TRAM.

An A-6E of the East Coast Intruder replacement training squadron, VA-42 Green Pawns, based at NAS Oceana, Virginia. (David F. Brown)

A KA-6D of VA-52 refuels an F-4J of VF-114 during the last combat cruise for both squadrons aboard USS KITTY HAWK (CVA-63) during 1972-73. All KA-6Ds assigned to VA-52 carried a Blue band around the rear fuselage. (Nick Waters)

There was an A-7 Shrike support on the first hop I flew in that period. One of the SAM sites locked on to him and fired a missile, which he apparently did not see. The SAM nailed him, but somehow he managed to eject. We didn't know anything about this, but when we went feet wet again, we flew right over the burning wreckage on the beach. He was picked up and taken to a POW camp. I saw him when the POWs were repatriated, and he said; "You ass! You almost ran over me! I was floating down in my chute when you came by so close that I could see the red lights in the cockpit!" Of course, we never saw him. We were going as fast as the airplane would go and the lights were off.

On the second or third night, we were given a target which was an airfield just outside of Haiphong. A Vigilante had been through that afternoon and taken pictures of Chinese transports offloading SAM missiles, still in their wooden shipping crates. When the picture was taken, there were several hundred of these things lined up along this long east-west runway. The North Vietnamese would bring their trucks in and load these things up for transport to their various SAM sites. This was a very lucrative target and we were very happy to get it! They loaded us with twenty-two Rockeyes and launched us.

The standard A-6 computer was suspect at best at that time and that night it didn't work at all, so it was a manual rangeline bomb release. The end of the runway was no more than seven or eight miles from the beach, so we flew up into Haiphong Harbor until we were abeam of the runway, turned left to 270 and were looking right down the runway. We were at 300 feet, going as fast

as we could...probably about 450 knots. I picked up the runway on the radar, called for a slight right turn...level the wings...steady up...it was night and no rough air. With a manual drop, you have a pre-determined manual rangeline set...that is, the computer is not dropping the bombs, you are dropping the bombs when the manual rangeline touches the target you intend to hit. In this case, we were dropping them in a long string and we wanted the first bomb to come off about 200 feet early. We were going to spread them the length of the runway.

I guess if I had to do it another hundred times, I could not do it any better. The bombs started coming off and almost immediately the airplane started rocking and rolling to the left and right. At the end of the run, we had to make a hard right turn because there was a big mountain on the left. A right turn is an unnatural act for an A-6 pilot, because of his restricted visibility out of the starboard side of he aircraft. He honked on something in excess of four Gs...no problem...I looked at the vertical speed indicator (VSI) and the airspeed indicator...no problem. We were coming around to a pre-determined escape heading. I looked out the right side of the airplane and, lo and behold, all those SAM missiles were doing strange and wonderful things, now that they were lit off by the Rockeyes. The rocket motors were blazing as they arced across the sky and slithered along the ground, blasting into hangars and other buildings. Naturally, this pleased me to no end and I punched the pilot on the arm and hollered, "Jeez! Lookit this shit!!" Bad mistake. He looked over and started enjoying the show while we were still in this hard right turn. Meanwhile, I had started dropping a little chaff in response to a SAM radar that was looking at us. I was still looking outside when the missile alert and the missile launch warnings went off at the same time. I looked back in the cockpit and discovered we were at 1,200 feet in a thirty degree bank, and still climbing. The missile was in the air at our dead six o'clock, which is the worst

This Intruder of VA-52 was damaged in a landing accident. The aircraft was lifted from NAS North Island by a CH-53E and delivered to NARF Alameda for rebuilding. Hydraulic failure resulted in a gear-up landing during the Summer of 1990. (U.S. Navy by PH1 Michael D.P. Flynn)

This A-6A of VMA (AW)-224 Bengals carries the special tail markings associated with Project Stormfury, a hurricane research and modification program run during 1970. (Dr. J.G. Handelman)

An A-6A Intruder of VA-52 coming aboard USS KITTY HAWK (CVA-63) after a 1972 combat mission. The Intruder has caught the number one wire, which undoubtedly did not make the LSO happy, since most LSOs feel that aiming for the number one wire is flirting with a ramp strike. (Nick Waters)

place in the world for one to come at you from. I called for a break down, and he rolls in 120 degrees of bank...we were now at 1,700 feet...and snaps on four and a half Gs...in the dark! Going through 900 feet, still dropping chaff, I called for him to level the wings. He rolled hard, using both stick and rudder, and we leveled off at 180 feet on the radar altimeter! About the same time, the missile went over the top of us and detonated about 600 yards in front of us, with a big White flash. Obviously, it was not our night to die.

On another mission, we caught a whole convoy of trucks bottled up on the coast road south of Thanh Hoa. In that area, the mountains come almost right down to the coast and it is real tough to move anywhere except on the road with a truck. The night before this mission, we had come down this road and dropped a bunch of mines in a narrow pass. This NVA convoy was about ten miles long, and the first truck had hit one of these mines. That stalled the whole convoy, and that's where we came in. I had already flown two hops that day, and was back in my state room, writing letters, when I was called to the ready room and advised that I was going on a third mission. They launched two aircraft, the lead was Rich Coleman, with BN Phil Hart. Ron Freed was my pilot. It was a rapid reaction mission...no brief...just get in the aircraft and fly. We were loaded with sixteen Rockeyes each and we flew in section until we were twenty miles off the beach. We were on the right wing and at that point we turned off the lights and started a right standard rate turn. Richie turned off his lights, got down in the dirt, and went through the pass ahead of us. We went through at about 800 feet because some of the rock outcroppings were pretty high. Once we were through the pass, we eased on down a little lower. There were no SAMs in the area, but it seemed like about every fourth

or fifth truck had a ZU-23 (quad-mounted 23MM AA gun). That made it pretty easy to see just where the trucks were. As we flew down the road, we knew that anywhere there was a red hose coming up at us, there was a truck! Richie dropped his, and we dropped ours and got out of there. The next day a Vigilante went through and we got credit for forty plus trucks destroyed.

During what I call "that period of misfortune which followed the Vietnam War," there was little funding for anything. The Congress saw that the military had two all-weather attack platforms, the Navy/Marine Corps A-6 Intruder and the USAF F-111. The F-111, of course, enjoyed the full support of the USAF and all its friends in congress, while the A-6 was the "Red-headed stepchild" of aviation...never acknowledged or called upon until it was time to kick someone's butt. The statement "we only need one all-weather attack aircraft in the U.S. arsenal" was circulated in Washington. The Navy took this seriously enough to suggest publicly that a fly-off between the two aircraft should take place. (The Navy had previously had its unhappy experience with the F-111, and eventually had cancelled its version of the General Dynamics bomber in favor of developing the F-14 Tomcat.)

A deal was struck to organize a three-part competition, to be held at NAS Oceana, Virginia. Part one would be pure bombing accuracy, using a matrix which included high speed, varying altitudes and dive angles, and day/night operations. The second, and more interesting, part of the competition was real-world, night, low level navigation and attack. Multiple targets in our local flying area, which included Virginia, West Virginia, Ohio, Tennessee, the Carolinas, and even up into Pennsylvania, were surveyed. Some of these targets were one-lane, wooden road bridges in deep ravines. Some were power plants that a blind man could find, and there was a lot of stuff in between. The aim

VMAT (AW) 202 was formed on 15 January 1968 and deactivated on 30 September 1986. A-6s assigned to VMAT (AW)-202 were marked with a Red fin and rudder and a Black two-headed imperial eagle. (Norman E. Taylor)

Ordnance crewmen load a multiple ejector rack (MER) pre-loaded with Mk 82 high drag bombs on the outboard wing pylon of an A-6.

An EA-6B Prowler of VAQ-138 Yellow Jackets. Prowlers in the Gulf were armed with Standard ARM and HARM anti-radiation missiles.

This VMAT (AW)-202 A-6A (BuNo 157003) was one of the last A-6As manufactured. All lettering on the tail was in Black, while the nose and tail tips of the drop tanks were Red. (Grumman)

points were very specific. It was not just "hit the bridge," it was hit the northeast corner of the bridge.

The scoring was done electronically. A team of engineers went to these targets and installed equipment which would be interrogated by a pod carried on the bomber. This pod contained an independent inertial navigation system and a computer which 'knew' all the ballistics of the weapons which could be carried on each airplane. When a bomb release pulse was sent to the bomb, via the commit switch, the pod compared the target position with that of the airplane, computed the airspeed, dive angle, and weapons ballistics of the weapons selected, and scored the hits.

All the runs were flown at night. Some were flown at 2,000 feet AGL, but the bulk of them were flown much lower. On most missions, you had to be faster than 400 knots and below 800 feet AGL, regardless of the terrain, in order to be scored. We asked the Air Force to fly the same targets as we did, and we volunteered to go to Mountain Home AFB and bomb their targets...and invited them to come to Oceana and fly our targets. Someone made the decision that separate targets would be used. Intelligence Officers from each service certified the other's targets to be of equal value in the proposed matrix. The third part of the competition was survivability in an electronic warfare environment and I can't disclose any of those details because they are classified.

The crew matrix included everyone from the Squadron CO right down to the guy who walked in the door last week. Every squadron at Oceana, on turnaround, was called upon to provide aircrews. That also included VA-42, the A-6 training squadron. Because of it's greater speed, the F-111 was adjudged to be more survivable, and that was no great surprise. The A-6 won the bombing competition. I was an instructor in the training squadron, and was called upon to fly two of the sorties. As I recall, the competition took about a month. The A-6 won the bombing competition by a fairly narrow margin...twenty feet or so, as I recall it...inside the F-111, which had flown its missions at Eglin AFB, Florida. The A-6 won the night attack competition by nearly fifty percent over the F-111 CEP. When the competition was

over, the powers-that-be in Washington looked at the test results and evidently did not see what they wanted or expected, so they declared the tests "inconclusive." The bottom line was that the A-6 remained in the fleet.

When I was CO of VA-55, I led a practice strike from about 200 miles north of Bermuda to Avon Park, Florida...a long, long way! We needed refueling, of course, and the Air Force was tasked to provide the gas. We rendezvoused off the coast of the Carolinas with three KC-135 tankers, six F-111s and two EF-111s. In my strike group were six A-6s and six F-18s, four configured as fighters and two as HARM shooters, (HARM is a radar homing missile used to attack SAM sites) and one EA-6B.

The controller of this inter-service strike group was an Air Force E-3 AWACS, call sign "Bandsaw," which was pre-positioned off the Florida coast. We had planned this mission two months prior at a meeting in Virginia Beach. The controller was a lady in the E-3 and when she asked me what my time on target (TOT) was going to be, I told her, "0400 straight up." She was more than just skeptical, she figured the best we could do would be plus or minus a few minutes. I told her that normal Navy policy was plus or minus 10 seconds. The argument continued until I finally suggested a bet of a case of Moosehead Beer. She said I couldn't get within 3 minutes. I suggested a minute and a half. She laughed and accepted and away we went, with me trying to figure how she would screw me out of that case of beer.

I asked for a time hack when we were still 200 miles off the coast, and that's when the F-111s started falling off like popcorn. One of them had a terrain following radar problem, another had a computer problem, and finally only two of them actually crossed the beach, and they were way off time. My first bomb hit the ground, and was called a bullseye by the guy on the ground scoring...at 0400 plus six seconds! That mission was a six hour round trip ride and I was looking forward to collecting that case of beer. I called her on the phone and she promised to ship it, but she never has.

An A-6A Intruder of VA-35 enroute to targets in Vietnam during 1968. The squadron's combat cruise lasted from January to July 1968, aboard USS ENTERPRISE. The Black Panthers also made combat cruises aboard USS CORAL SEA (69-70) and USS AMERICA (72-73). (U.S. Navy by LTJG W.G. Taylor)

This A-6E Intruder of VA-196 Main Battery carries CAG markings of CVW-14 during December of 1977. The air wing was assigned to USS ENTERPRISE at that time. (Shinichi Ohtaki)

An A-6A of VA-35 lands aboard USS NIMITZ on 27 July 1981. The aircraft is carrying a MER on each inboard wing pylon and an external fuel tank on the centerline station. (U.S. Navy)

This A-6E (BuNo 157009) of VA-176 Thunderbolts on the ramp at NAS Oceana, Virginia, was assigned to USS FRANKLIN D. ROOSEVELT during June of 1974. The equipment bay door is hinged at the rear. (Norman E. Taylor)

LT Ladd Wheeler

...graduated from the University of Kansas during 1982, with a degree in Chemical Engineering, gained with the assistance of a Reserve Officers Training Command (ROTC) scholarship. Since his eyes were not good enough to allow him to pass the physical for pilot training, he decided that Naval Flight Officer (NFO) training offered the best opportunity for a person who wanted a military flying career in the rear (or side) seat of a carrier based aircraft.

After basic training at Pensacola, he was given the option of going to jets or props. He chose jets and asked for the A-6 in particular. Upon completion of intermediate and advanced NFO training, he was selected for A-6s. He was assigned to the West Coast A-6 replacement training squadron, VA-128, where he began operational training during January of 1984.

My interview with Ladd Wheeler took place at the Naval Air Test Center, NAS Patuxent River, Maryland, in September of 1990. He was assigned there after graduating from the U.S. Naval Test Pilot School (USNTPS). He had recently been selected Naval Flight Officer of The Year and received word that he had been selected for Lieutenant Commander well in advance of the "zone." (One sure measure of the state of an officer's career is whether or not he is promoted prior to the standard time in grade. There is no question about being promoted or not......if you are not promoted, or "passed over," you are not long for the service. On the other hand, being promoted early marks you as a possible rising star, someone to be watched more closely and considered for tough and/or prestigious assignments, whose successful completion further enhances your career prospects). All this made it apparent that Ladd Wheeler is a bright and highly motivated Naval Officer. He is also quite articulate and his comments on his flying career, and the A-6 in particular, make interesting reading.

I completed training with VA-128 during September of 1984 and was assigned to VA-165 Boomers, one of eight A-6 squadrons at NAS Whidbey Island, Washington. Over the three years that I was fortunate enough to be associated with them, The Boomers experienced nothing but success. This success was driven primarily by the senior officers, especially the squadron commander, CAPT Bob "Buff" Knowles, and XO (later commander) CAPT John "Scraps" Scrapper. Buff is an NFO and he really taught me how to run the system. I got to fly with Scraps for a year and a half of my tour and that experience greatly enhanced my knowledge of carrier aviation.

On my first cruise, I was assigned to the USS KITTY HAWK (CV-63), which was home-ported in San Diego. With the exception of the Boomers and VAQ-130 Zappers, the EA-6B squadron, all the other squadrons from the Air Wing were based in California. I was lucky enough to begin my assignment at a time when the KITTY HAWK was commencing its turn-around cycle for the air wing training. I saw all of the development that goes into the training of an air wing, including visual weapons detachments at Fallon and REFTRAS (refresher training) designed to allow the carrier and air wing to get to know each other during a combination of one and two week deployments off the Southern California coast. Soon after, we left on our first KITTY HAWK cruise to the Western Pacific and Indian Ocean.

My training at Whidbey Island included a lot of night flying. In fact, for every day flight, there was a corresponding night flight. These flights were through the Cascade and the Olympic mountains. When you ingress the mountains in the A-6, you really come to grips with your capabilities as an Intruder crew. You are flying 100% self-contained, with the BN supplying terrain and steering information to the pilot minutes ahead of the airplane. You "talk" to the pilot on to his radar-generated display, which allows him to "see" a three dimensional view of what is in front of the airplane, while flying on instruments. Only once, during that type of night flying, did I ever look outside the cockpit and I'll never do it again! It was a frightening experience to see the trees and rocks whizzing past so close! I would just as soon concentrate on the business at hand and keep my head in the cockpit.

When you are flying around the boat at night, your mission becomes that of support system for the pilot. You are a talking attitude indicator. It seems that, no matter how beautiful it is up at 20,000 feet, when you get down to 1,200 feet on your approach to the ship, it is always dark, there is always a cloud layer above you and you feel like you are flying downhill when you know you are straight and level. Pilots seem to be more susceptible to vertigo than BNs...at least, that has been my experience and I believe it is because BNs rely totally on the instruments with little or no hands-on/seat-of-the-pants feedback. Pilots, on the other hand, are bombarded by sensory inputs which makes it tougher for them to believe what the instruments are telling them. Not only do they have to look outside, they also have the stick and throttle in hand and are getting all kinds of feedback from the airframe. When a pilot tells you he has vertigo, you have got to respect what he is saying and really try to help him overcome it,

LT Ladd Wheeler inspects a load of live Mk 82 bombs prior to launch from USS KITTY HAWK during 1987 contingency operations in the Indian Ocean. (LT Wheeler)

A pair of VA-165 Intruders prepare to complete a 'Buddy Bombing' timed release of Mk 82 bombs during power projection (fire power) demonstration for the Sultan of Brunei during 1987. (LT Ladd Wheeler)

This A-6E (BuNo 158529) of VA-34 Blue Blasters chocked on the ramp at NAS Oceana, on 14 November 1974 was assigned to USS JOHN F. KENNEDY. The aircraft is carrying 300 gallon fuel tanks on the outboard wing pylon and centerline station. (Norman E. Taylor)

An A-6E (BuNo 157027) of VMA (AW)-533 on the ramp at Offutt Air Force Base, Nebraska on 3 December 1982. The drop tank fin is in the same checker design as the aircraft rudder. (Norman E. Taylor)

because you are in about the worst place in the world to have vertigo when trying to land on a carrier at night. Weather or no weather, it is just plain dark!

LT Dan Mabry was my JO pilot. He was very talented behind the boat and he never scared me (although he may have scared himself)! Scraps was rock-solid...never a surprise. I do recall one night though that got a little frustrating, if not hairy. The A-6 has a hook snubber, which keeps downward pressure on the tailhook when it is down. If that pressure ever bleeds off, the hook is subject to bouncing over the wire on landing. Scraps and I had that happen one night, and it resulted in several "bolters" and go-arounds before catching a wire. A procedure used when you absolutely are unable to catch a wire is to have deck personnel get rolls of toilet paper and stack them up under the wires, thereby raising the wires enough to catch the hook. Fortunately, that was not exercised.

We spent a good deal of the latter half of 1985 on station at 20 degrees north latitude at the mouth of the Persian Gulf. It was a rewarding cruise, in that it gave everyone a chance to spend a lot of time building their experience base around the boat. We flew a lot of "what if" scenarios and really learned to use the A-6 as the projection of the power for the air wing.

The second cruise aboard KITTY HAWK began in January of 1987. Once again we headed for WestPac and the Indian Ocean, though the plan was for us to ultimately make an "around the world cruise." Eventually we did do that, but not without considerable delay, once again because of events in the Middle East. On 17 May, we passed through the Suez Canal. This was a memorable date because of another event, one which would delay us in our journey. The USS STARK was hit by an Exocet Missile launched from an Iraqi aircraft. We were held on station in the Mediterranean Sea as the contingency carrier, while another carrier hustled West to take our place in the Indian Ocean. Five weeks were spent in the Med, before finally heading home to the United States. We left the KITTY HAWK in Philadelphia, where it was to undergo a complete rework at the Service Life Extension Facility (SLEP). My two cruises in three years comprised a total of 330 days underway and 1,100 hours of operational flying in the A-6. Since leaving the fleet, I have logged an additional 700 hours, divided among twenty-five different aircraft types. That reflects the Test Pilot School experience, where you are given the chance to fly in a great variety of aircraft in the armed forces inventory. This allows you to "mission relate" while testing various aircraft and weapons systems.

On my first cruise with the Boomers, I was a Junior Officer (JO) and we had a lot of great JOs in that squadron. Sixteen of the thirty-two officers were bachelors, so you can imagine the atmosphere in the ready room. One memorable "non-event" was a quick reaction strike that three A-6 JO crews organized against Midway Island during our transition to the Indian Ocean. Midway just happened to be within striking distance of the carrier, so we planned and executed this mission with the permission, although not the participation, of our Senior officers. The Midway natives were caught off-guard by our three Intruders, appearing from "nowhere," making a low-level dry bomb run, and disappearing over the horizon. Midway's only defense were the large flocks of gooney birds that launched in response to our raid. We were fortunate to avoid them, as a bird-strike would have ruined someone's day! It was a heady experience for a bunch of brand-new fleet aviators. The experiences of the balance of that cruise sort of all run together. There were no "big events"...no traumatic experiences. Just the day after day excitement of flying on and off the carrier, planning practice missions, and getting to know the Intruder better.

Prior to my second cruise, I was asked if I would be interested in being the Squadron Commander's Bombadier Navigator. Naturally, I accepted. The primary benefit of this experience was that of direct leadership, at a fairly junior level, of large formations of aircraft on contingency air wing strikes. I was the navigator, of course, but I was also the Skipper's assistant in keeping track of the big picture. Scraps was a very talented pilot and he didn't have any trouble doing this by himself, but every little bit of assistance helped. These were sixteen to twenty airplane strikes, with diverse aircraft types, including F-14s, A-7s, E-2s and, of course, A-6s. The knowledge gained, the airmanship demonstrated by CAPT Scrapper, the opportunity to handle fairly dynamic scenarios and to do that without making a mistake (when you have that many people depending on you, you really have to be meticulous in planning and execution)...all combined to make this a very memorable cruise. Scraps was somewhat of a character when it came to planning. We would sit down for hours on end in mission planning on the carrier, working out these highly integrated strike plans for multitudes of aircraft. He would draw cards out, color code them and have them all lined up in the order of the events...then never carry them with him on the mission. He would have all the information committed to memory!

One of the missions that the A-6 flies is that of tanker. The tanker mission is particularly important when a pilot has a problem coming aboard and needs more fuel in hurry. The airborne recovery tanker is usually at medium altitude over the boat, but if someone is really having a problem, the tanker will come down and "hawk" the guy.

An A-6A of VA-34 Blue Blaster uses a buddy store refueling pod to refuel an RA-5C Vigilante photographic reconnaissance aircraft during July of 1971. (U.S. Navy)

A KA-6D Intruder tanker of VA-34 refuels a pair of A-7 Corsair IIs of VA-46 Clansmen while operating from USS JOHN F. KENNEDY in the Med during April of 1973. (U.S. Navy)

A KA-6D Intruder tanker of VA-196 is positioned on the starboard bow catapult aboard USS CORAL SEA during operations in the Indian Ocean in February of 1980. The wing leading edge slats are fully deployed. (U.S. Navy by PH2 James C. Brown)

The tail markings on VA-165 Boomers Intruders became more colorful during 1974 and included a Green delta, a Gold star and a White knight chess piece. These A-6As were enroute to targets during Operation MIDLINK '74, held in the Indian Ocean, on 17 November 1974. (U.S. Navy by PHCS R.L. Lawson)

The technique calls for the tanker to be in exactly the right position, so that the Air Boss can tell the troubled aviator to look up at his one o'clock, for instance, and he should see the tanker. That was one of CAPT Scrapper's favorite missions...the last night recovery tanker. He used to say that, "Death, taxes, and the last night recovery tanker were the only things for sure in life." The last night recovery tanker always launched!

In my two tours, we never lost an airplane from the Air Wing. Considering the level of tension and the demands placed upon the crews, this was a testament to their professionalism. It is also, obviously, a testament to very good aircraft maintenance. We did lose a few people from the flight deck crews. The flight deck is a very dangerous place during air ops, and I never spent any more time there than was absolutely necessary!

The Boomer tour ended in December of 1987, upon selection to USNTPS, where I was a member of class 94. I graduated in December of 1988 and was assigned to Pax River's Strike Aircraft Test Directorate, where I have been conducting tests on the A-6 primarily, although I have a NATOPS F-14 qualification and have done some F-14 testing. I have also been involved with efforts for the Navy's A-6 follow-on attack aircraft, the A-12 Avenger II. My next assignment will be as a department head with a West Coast operational A-6 squadron.

Test work with the A-6 involved mainly the advancements in avionics. These advancements, by themselves, are enough to keep you busy 365 days a year...just keeping up with the software and the available hardware that can be put into an airframe to supplement its operational mission. The A-6 is about maxed out in the hardware line, however as the ordnance-carrying platform for Navy Attack, every time something new comes along in ordnance, you have to integrate it with the A-6. In the last two years while working at Strike, I have helped to integrate the Standoff Land Attack Missile (SLAM) and I am currently testing Walleye, which is a potent weapon that has been carried by other fleet aircraft, but not the A-6. The Intruder has been around for a long time, and in most cases, it is well beyond what it's 1950 designers envisioned. With that in mind, the Boeing Military Aircraft Company was contracted to design, develop, and test a new wing for the A-6 which will extend the life of the Intruder well into the next century. This new wing is built of composites and is essentially unbreakable. It was designed to interface directly with the existing A-6 airframe, but with load dispersing qualities which will reduce fatigue of the old airframes. The new wing was required to be aerodynamically and structurally identical to the old wing. Boeing's mis-

sion was made more difficult by this requirement, since all the "lumps and bumps" associated with early wing-building technology directly affected aerodynamic performance of the wing. This performance had to be duplicated on what is essentially a smooth wing. All of the existing and proposed ordnance loads had to be certified as well. To date we are about 2/3 of the way complete with testing the wing. On 29 October, I completed the first all-Navy ordnance test with LT Russ Knight. We dropped twenty-eight Mk 82 bombs off the new wings, with no anomalies noted. We have since conducted fifteen additional successful tests, with about three more to go before it is certified to the metal wing base line capabilities. The new wing has yet to be evaluated in the Carrier Suitability environment, and some checks and balances of the Boeing flight test program will be flown by Navy aircrews to validate BMAC's. The goal is to get the wing completely evaluated and certified to the full limits of it's capabilities as soon as possible.

Ladd Wheeler's approach to our interview was very professional and, like most airmen, he did not dwell on the dangers of his profession. Carrier aviation is dangerous, and so is test flying. During my visit, I had been scheduled to speak to CAPT Steve "Axel" Hazelrigg, a very senior A-6 pilot who was scheduled to assume command of Strike Aircraft Directorate at NATC. Two weeks before my visit Hazelrigg and LCDR Bill "Catfish" Davis were testing an ordnance shape on an A-6. They were at 5,000 feet, doing 520 knots. Axel had initiated a test sequence of planned stick transitions when something in the back of the airplane came apart. The Ground instrumentation showed rapid transition to negative G flight and ground impact only seconds later. Davis somehow managed to eject. Hazelrigg did not. As of this writing, Davis is rapidly recovering from extensive injuries and Hazelrigg is mourned by his contemporaries.

The Naval Aviator's ability to make light of his more hair-raising experiences is often reflected in the call signs they take, or are given by their fellow crews. "Axel" had acquired his while a junior officer. Coming aboard the carrier one night, he had a high rate of descent and contacted the deck in an extreme wing down attitude, breaking off one of the main mounts and boltering in the process. He was now airborne with just two wheels. He eventually landed in the barricade, but from that night on, he was "Axel." Ladd Wheeler acquired the callsign "Paul Bunyan" after his excursion through some trees at the end of the Pax River runway, while riding the back seat of an TF/A-18. It was on a takeoff. The airplane was heavy and a loss of power at

An A-6 of VA-52 flies over Southern California enroute to the target range with a load of inert bombs during a practice mission from USS KITTY HAWK on 23 March 1979. (U.S. Navy by PHC Arthur E. Legare)

An A-6E Intruder of VA-115 takes off for a 27 July 1982 mission over Japan. It is armed with a practice Standard ARM anti-radiation missile on the inboard pylon. The Standard ARM is used for the anti-SAM Iron Hand mission. (Shinichi Ohtaki)

A pair of A-6Es of VA-196 on the deck edge elevator of USS CORAL SEA. The aircraft in the foreground has the ram air turbine (RAT) on the port wing root deployed. Markings include a Red/Orange stripe on the tail and a Black spade inside a Red/Orange circle on fuselage. (Grumman)

This A-6E of VA-75 is outfitted for maximum range with five 300 gallon external fuel tanks. This configuration gave the Intruder an endurance of over six hours and a range of 1,394 nautical miles. (David F. Brown)

This A-6A of VMA (AW)-332 Polkadots carries a tactical camouflage consisting of Blue Gray over White with White codes. The only colors on the aircraft were the national insignia and warning markings.

a critical point had them headed for the ground. The pilot was looking at the instruments when Ladd saw the ground coming up. He hollered and the pilot reacted quickly, going to 50 units of Angle of Attack and turning the Hornet into a rocket ship. Unfortunately though, not before trees had removed both slats, major portions of the flaps, and the entire port stabilator! There were also big pieces of trees sucked into both engines. The flight control computer somehow managed to compensate for all of that and they were able to land the aircraft without further incident. That was a testament to both the integrity of the F/A-18 and to the talent of the pilots. As Ladd Wheeler said, "That was the longest two minutes and fifty second flight I ever want to experience!"

These A-6Es of VA-34 carry subdued unit markings which began to appear during the early 1980s. The Intruder in the foreground has the Ram Air Turbine (RAT) deployed. (David F.Brown)

This A-6E of VA-65 carries another variation of the subdued markings used during April of 1984. The air group, carrier, and squadron markings are in Pale Gray, while the aircraft numbers and Navy are in Black. (David F.Brown)

This KA-6D of VA-176 at Offutt AFB, Nebraska, carries another style of low viz markings. The blade antenna behind the canopy is for the Omega navigation system. Omega was fitted solely to tanker versions of the Intruder. (George Cockle via Norman E. Taylor.)

A KA-6D of VA-55 Warhorses aboard USS CORAL SEA in the Mediterranean during the Spring of 1986. During this deployment, VA-55 participated in attacks on Libyan military targets in response to Libyan sponsored terrorist attacks on civilian targets. (U.S. Navy)

A KA-6D tanker of VA-34 aboard USS AMERICA during November of 1985. Beginning in November of 1984 Grumman, St. Augustine Corp. began a program to update the Intruder tanker fleet with new fuel cells, new wiring, new avionics and a bulkhead replacement. The updated KA-6Ds are identified by their capability to carry five 400 gallon wing tanks. (Author)

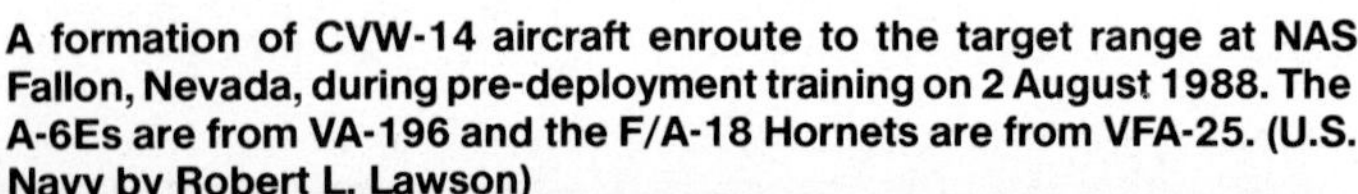

A formation of CVW-14 aircraft enroute to the target range at NAS Fallon, Nevada, during pre-deployment training on 2 August 1988. The A-6Es are from VA-196 and the F/A-18 Hornets are from VFA-25. (U.S. Navy by Robert L. Lawson)

An A-6E (TRAM) Intruder during testing at NAS Patuxent River, Maryland, on 2 November 1981. To record tests a camera platform has been mounted on the air intake. The addition of the Target Recognition Attack Multisensor (TRAM) system to the A-6 provided it with capabilities which would extend the Intruder's operational life time into the 1990s. (D.F. Brown)

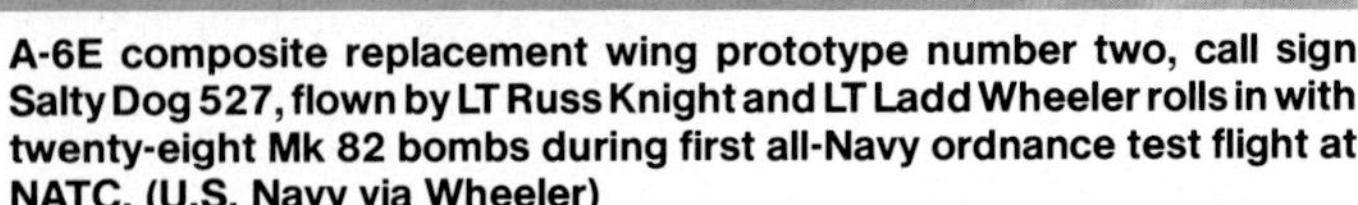

A-6E composite replacement wing prototype number two, call sign Salty Dog 527, flown by LT Russ Knight and LT Ladd Wheeler rolls in with twenty-eight Mk 82 bombs during first all-Navy ordnance test flight at NATC. (U.S. Navy via Wheeler)

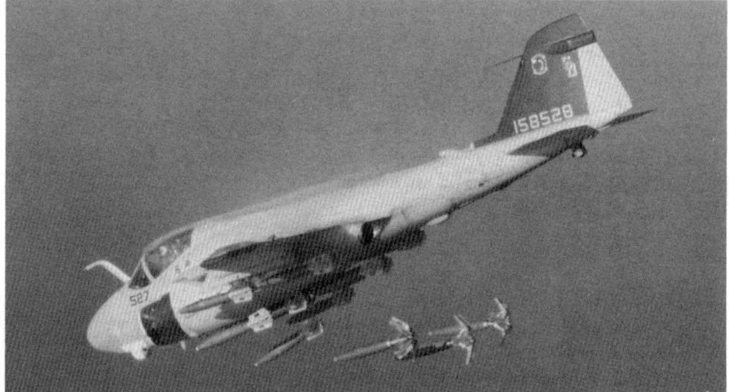

Salty Dog 527, with pilot CDR Bill Washer and BN LCDR Ken Smolana conduct a Mk 82 high drag weapons release test. The shock-induced vapors over the fuselage and wing are indicative of transonic speeds. (U.S. Navy)

Salty Dog 527, loaded with twenty-eight Mk 20 Rockeye CBUs, on the Strike Aircraft Test Directorate ramp. Although relatively old, the Rockeye is still one of the most effective munitions carried by the Intruder and it saw wide use in Operation DESERT STORM. (U.S. Navy)

SD 527, loaded with four MK 84 Laser Guided Bombs (LGBs) rolls in during Navy validation testing of the A-6E composite replacement wing. Cameras are mounted on the aircraft centerline station and within the TRAM turret in the nose. (U.S. Navy)

An EA-6A (BuNo 156989) of VMCJ-1 on the ramp at MCAS Iwakuni, Japan during 1973. The engine compartment is open and the engine removed in preparation for an engine change. (H. Nagakubo via Norman E. Taylor)

Jammers

Electronic warfare was born during the Second World War II, although it was limited to noise jamming of radio frequencies. Jamming of radar-directed AAA began during the Korean War, shortly after that threat became significant. Air war tacticians recognized that the electronic spectrum would present offensive opportunities and defensive challenges sufficient to demand dedicated electronic mission aircraft. The first of these were modified versions of the North American TB-25J and the Douglas F3D (later EF-10) and AD-5. The latter two were the first to carry externally mounted jamming pods.

Introduction of the radar guided SA-2 Surface to air missile accentuated the need for a sophisticated aircraft dedicated solely to the EW mission. The first SA-2 sites were detected in Cuba during the Cuban Missile Crisis, but the first truly integrated air defense use of SAMs was in Vietnam. The first U.S. airplane lost to a SAM was an F-4C Phantom II , which was shot down south of Hanoi on 24 July 1965. At this point, it is fair to say that the U.S. was behind their principle opponent in the battle for electronic domination of the battlefield.

Work had begun on the electronic warfare version of the Intruder in 1961, under the designation A2F-1H. By the time the aircraft made its first flight during 1963, DOD had changed the aircraft designation system and it flew as the EA-6A. The principle airframe differences between the A-6A and the EA-6A included; an eight inch plug behind the radome to increase the capacity for electronic gear,

This EA-6A Intruder of VMAQ-2 Playboys was home-based at MCAS Cherry Point, and was on deployment to MCAS Iwakuni, Japan, on 14 June 1978. The aircraft carries jammer pods on the outboard pylons and 300 gallon fuel tanks on the inboard and centerline pylons. (Shinichi Ohtaki)

elimination of the wingtip speed brakes, addition of a pod on top of the vertical fin to house antennas and the addition of a stores station on the outboard wing panels, which were strengthened for this purpose.

Because of their experience in the electronic warfare mission, the EA-6A was assigned to the Marines. Early versions were equipped with off-the-shelf detection and countermeasures equipment and were deployed to Danang, Vietnam during 1966, assigned to VMCJ-1. EA-6As continued flying combat until the end of the Vietnam War, although a constant upgrading of the electronics suite resulted in a much different aircraft by the end of the war.

The computers that are the heart of ECM equipment were becoming faster, more compact and more reliable, but the electronic battlefield expanded so rapidly that it outstripped the ability of the single Electronic Warfare Officer on the EA-6A to cope. Additionally, the installation of new equipment soon exceeded the load-carrying capability of the EA-6A airframe. The Navy and Grumman (independently) had foreseen this even before the EA-6A had gone into squadron service and when Grumman proposed the four-seat EA-6B during 1964, the Navy quickly awarded contracts for further study.

Design 128J added fifty-four inches to the standard A-6A fuselage to accommodate two additional crew members. The aircraft was designated the EA-6B and the fifteenth A-6A (BuNo 149481) was modified to this configuration, although without the electronics. The EA-6B made its first flight on 25 May 1968, with Don King at the controls. The second example (BuNo 149479) first flew during August of 1968, and this aircraft did most of the airborne systems tests.

This EA-6A of VMAQ-2 carried low visibility markings during 1978, which consisted of subdued shades of Gray for all markings, which remained full size. The fin tip radome housed ECM reconnaissance antennas. (Shinichi Ohtaki)

An EA-6A of VAQ-209 on the ramp at NAS Norfolk, Virginia during April of 1981. The EA-6A has an extra wing store pylon, outboard of the wing fold line, and an extra fence on top of the wing. The protective cover on the jammer pod is Red. (D.F. Brown)

A third modified A-6A (BuNo 148615) did not fly and spent most of its life in the Grumman anechoic chamber at Calverton. Five pre-production test aircraft were built. Operational testing did not begin until early 1970, with BIS trials and Carrier Qualifications being conducted aboard USS MIDWAY. The first production EA-6Bs were delivered to VAQ-129, the EA-6B training squadron, in October of 1970. The EA-6B entered squadron service in time to support the final air battles over North Vietnam and has seen considerable service in the years following Vietnam, including service in the Gulf War.

This EA-6A of VAQ-33 Firebirds at NAS Norfolk, Virginia, carries ALE-41 pods on the outboard pylon, ALQ-76 pods on the midwing pylons and a centerline fuel tank. (D.F. Brown)

An EA-6A (BuNo 156991) of VMCJ-2 on the ramp at Kelly Air Force Base, Texas, on 13 November 1971. The aircraft carries three ALQ-76 jamming pods and two 300 gallon fuel tanks. The canopy was outlined in Black. (Norman E. Taylor)

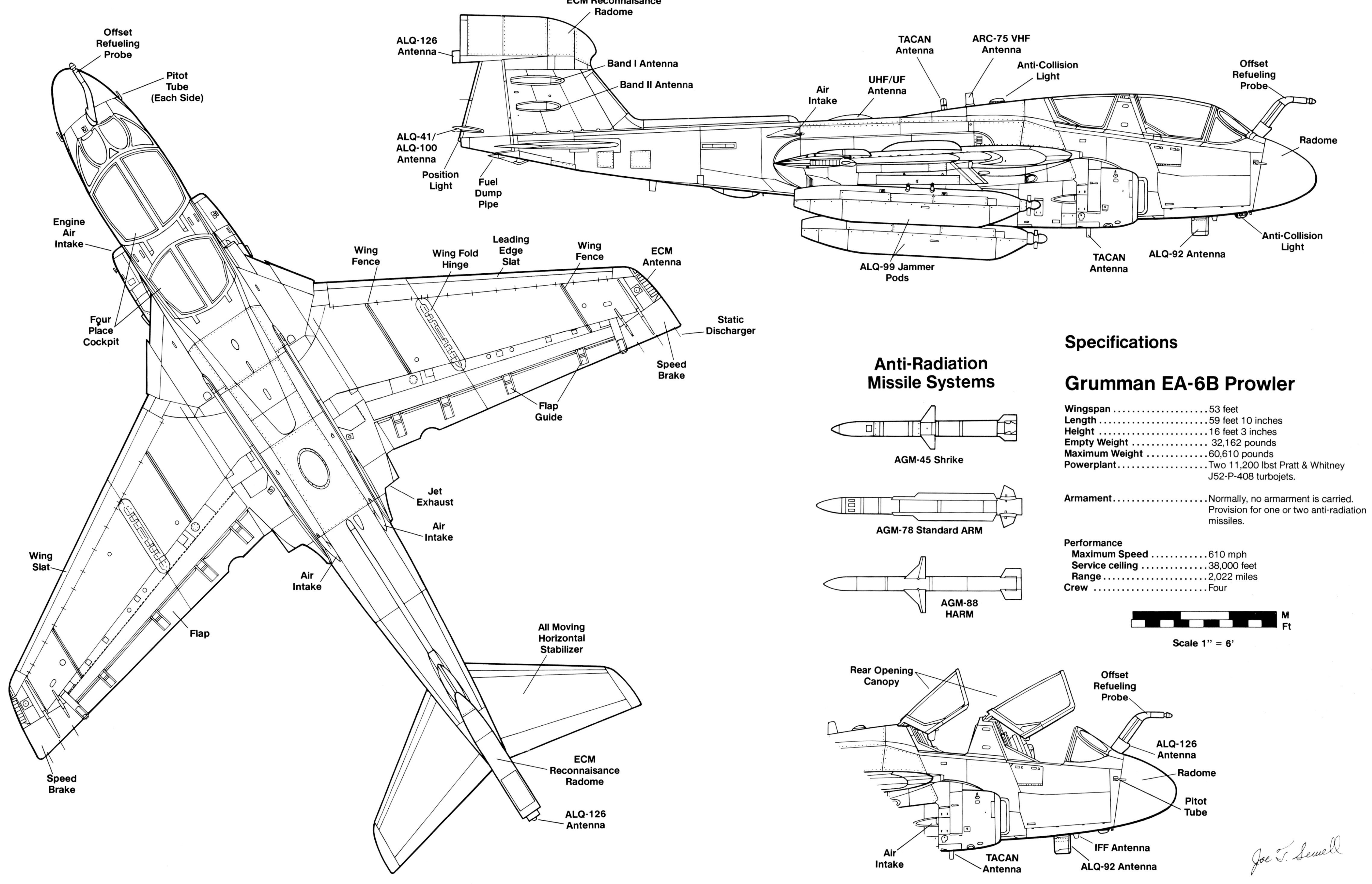

Offset Refueling Probe
Pitot Tube (Each Side)
ECM Reconnaisance Radome
ALQ-126 Antenna
Band I Antenna
Band II Antenna
TACAN Antenna
ARC-75 VHF Antenna
Anti-Collision Light
Air Intake
UHF/UF Antenna
Offset Refueling Probe
Radome
ALQ-41/ALQ-100 Antenna
Position Light
Fuel Dump Pipe
Engine Air Intake
Four Place Cockpit
Wing Fence
Wing Fold Hinge
Leading Edge Slat
Wing Fence
ECM Antenna
Static Discharger
Speed Brake
Flap Guide
ALQ-99 Jammer Pods
TACAN Antenna
ALQ-92 Antenna
Anti-Collision Light
Wing Slat
Jet Exhaust
Air Intake
Air Intake
Flap
Speed Brake
All Moving Horizontal Stabilizer
ECM Reconnaisance Radome
ALQ-126 Antenna
Anti-Radiation Missile Systems
AGM-45 Shrike
AGM-78 Standard ARM
AGM-88 HARM
Specifications
Grumman EA-6B Prowler
Wingspan . . . . 53 feet
Length . . . . 59 feet 10 inches
Height . . . . 16 feet 3 inches
Empty Weight . . . . 32,162 pounds
Maximum Weight . . . . 60,610 pounds
Powerplant . . . . Two 11,200 lbst Pratt & Whitney J52-P-408 turbojets.
Armament . . . . Normally, no armarment is carried. Provision for one or two anti-radiation missiles.
Performance
  Maximum Speed . . . . 610 mph
  Service ceiling . . . . 38,000 feet
  Range . . . . 2,022 miles
Crew . . . . Four
M
Ft
Scale 1" = 6'
Rear Opening Canopy
Offset Refueling Probe
ALQ-126 Antenna
Radome
Pitot Tube
Air Intake
TACAN Antenna
IFF Antenna
ALQ-92 Antenna
Joe T. Sewell

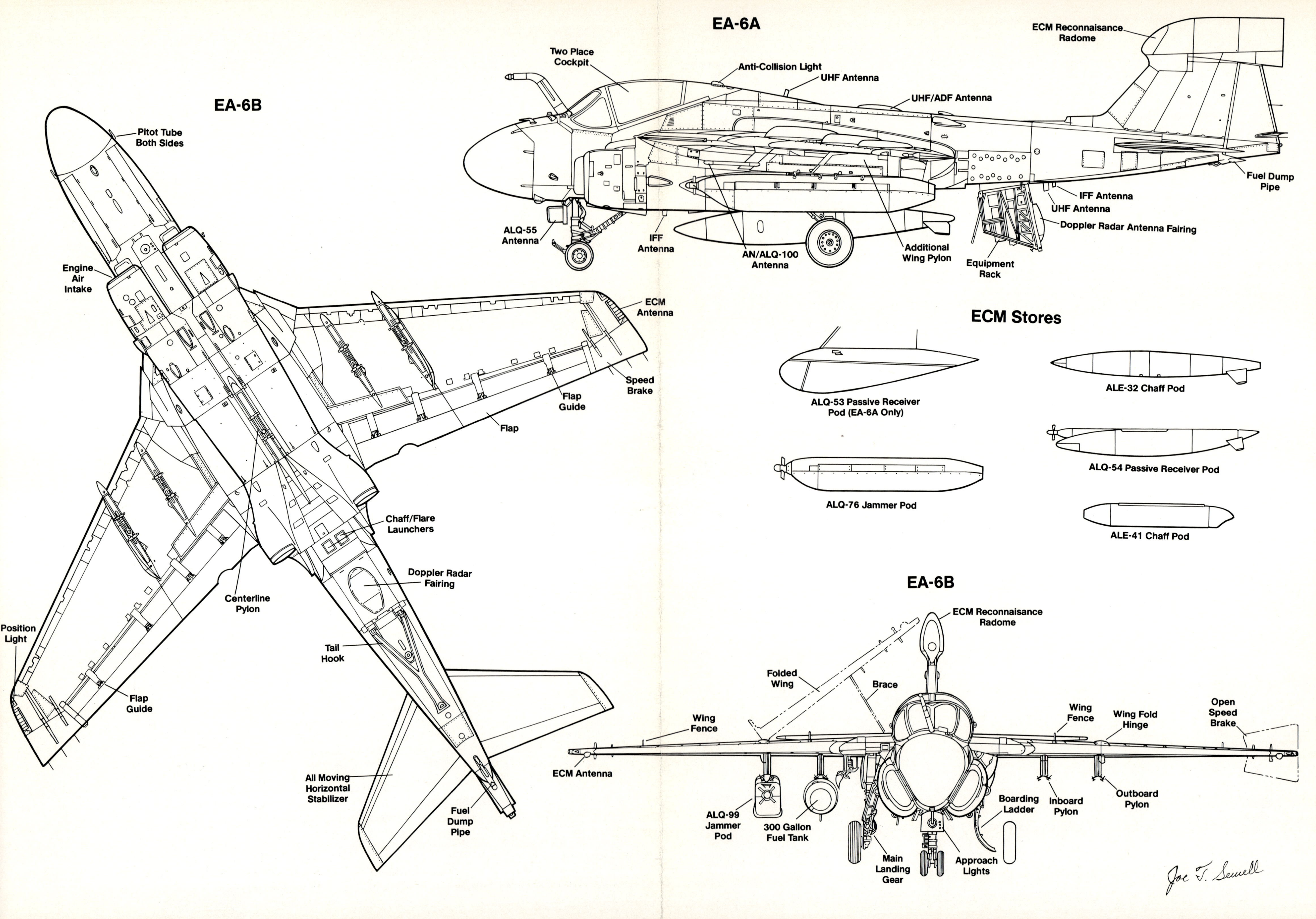

EA-6A
EA-6B
ECM Reconnaisance Radome
Two Place Cockpit
Anti-Collision Light
UHF Antenna
UHF/ADF Antenna
Pitot Tube Both Sides
Fuel Dump Pipe
IFF Antenna
UHF Antenna
Doppler Radar Antenna Fairing
ALQ-55 Antenna
IFF Antenna
AN/ALQ-100 Antenna
Additional Wing Pylon
Equipment Rack
Engine Air Intake
ECM Antenna
Speed Brake
Flap Guide
Flap
ECM Stores
ALQ-53 Passive Receiver Pod (EA-6A Only)
ALE-32 Chaff Pod
ALQ-76 Jammer Pod
ALQ-54 Passive Receiver Pod
ALE-41 Chaff Pod
Chaff/Flare Launchers
Doppler Radar Fairing
Centerline Pylon
Position Light
Tail Hook
Flap Guide
All Moving Horizontal Stabilizer
Fuel Dump Pipe
EA-6B
ECM Reconnaisance Radome
Folded Wing
Brace
Wing Fence
Wing Fence
Wing Fold Hinge
Open Speed Brake
ECM Antenna
ALQ-99 Jammer Pod
300 Gallon Fuel Tank
Main Landing Gear
Approach Lights
Boarding Ladder
Inboard Pylon
Outboard Pylon
Joe T. Sewell

An EA-6A of Reserve Squadron VAQ-309 Axemen, home based at NAS Whidbey Island, Washington. The extra scoop just forward of the VAQ-309 logo on the fuselage is for cooling the AN/ALQ-55 electronics. (Don Linn via D.F. Brown)

An EA-6A (BuNo 151600) of VMAQ-4 Seahawks on final approach for landing at Nellis Air Force Base, Nevada, after a 24 July 1990, Green Flag mission. In addition to its jammer pods, the aircraft carries a sensor pod on the midwing pylon. (Ted Carlson)

An EA-6B of VAQ-136, which served aboard USS MIDWAY and USS AMERICA, carrying the marking of both carriers on the fuselage above the NAVY. Normally, the squadron would deploy a detachment to each ship. (Shinichi Ohtaki)

An EA-6B of VAQ-129 Vikings, home based at Whidbey Island. VAQ-129 is the West Coast Fleet Replacement Squadron, and trains all pilots and electronic countermeasures officers (ECMO) for the EA-6B. The EA-6B carries a crew of four. (George Cockle via Norman E. Taylor)

(Left) An EA-6B at the Naval Air Test Center prior to fleet introduction. It carries three AN/ALQ-99 Tactical Jamming Pods. The pod on the inboard station is one of the original low band series, identified by its wider bottom profile. (U.S. Navy via Norman E. Taylor)

An EA-6B of VMAQ-2 Playboys on the taxiway at NAS Glenview, Ill., on 28 January 1990. The aircraft carries a mix of low-vis Gray markings with a Black Marines and squadron insignia. (Nathan Leong)

An EA-6B Prowler of VAQ-129 taxies in at NAS Glenview on 14 January 1990. The aircraft carries NAVY/MARINES markings indicating it is assigned to the Reserve program. (Nathan Leong)

This EA-6B Prowler of VAQ-130 on the ramp at NAS South Weymouth on 17 May 1975, is configured with four underwing 300 gallon fuel tanks and a jammer pod on the centerline station. (Norm Taylor)

Modern Combat

One of the primary differences in combat today is that many of the enemies of the United States espouse terrorism as one of their accepted tactics against the west. Terrorism recognizes no non-combatants. In fact, its targets are most often unarmed and defenseless civilians. Under those circumstances, many of the participants in this undeclared (as yet) war are unwilling to be quoted for attribution, fearing reprisals against their families by terrorists. That has not prevented many of them talking about their experiences over Lebanon and Libya. They just refused to be identified by name.

My first deployment was with VA-85, aboard USS FOR-RESTAL. We made an Eastern Med/IO (Mediterranean Sea/Indian Ocean) cruise from May to November of 1982. We actually assisted in putting the Marines in Beirut during June 1982. When we returned from that cruise, we were expecting a year turn-around, since the ship was scheduled to go to the shipyard for overhaul. Well, the ship got a rest, but we didn't. About three days before Christmas, when I was preparing to go on leave, the skipper came into the ready room and gave us the news that we would deploy aboard USS JOHN F. KENNEDY (CV-67), beginning with workups in February. This was the first test of the all Grumman Air Wing. We had two A-6 squadrons (VA-75 and VA-85) and two F-14 squadrons (VF-11 and VF-31), with no A-7s or F/A-18s. This was John Lehman's baby (former Secretary of the Navy, John Lehman, whose Naval Reserve job was pretending to be an A-6 B/N). This gave us high visibility and, because we were trying to prove a concept, a long workup period. The workups didn't end until our late September deployment. The deployment began with a trip to South America. Our first port of call was Rio de Janiero, and we had just pulled out when the Marine barracks in Beirut was blown up, with some 200 Marines being killed in the attack. We got the message to 'buster' over there, so the Captain put the pedal to the metal. We arrived in late October of 1983. This turned out to be a seven and a half month cruise. We shared the duty initially with USS EISENHOWER and then with USS INDEPENDENCE. The duty consisted of flying and standing 5, 10, or 15 minute alerts (alert aircraft are usually fighter, attack and tanker assets manned on the flight deck and situated so that they can launch on very short notice when needed), and we usually alternated on a daily basis with INDEPENDENCE. One day on alert, one day flying.

The flying for us consisted primarily of tankers for the F-14s and anti-surface warfare (ASUW) missions, in which we protected the gun line off of Lebanon. We had a bunch of small boys, (destroyers and frigates) as well as the USS NEW JERSEY (BB-62), which would come in close to the beach and fire their guns at targets inland in support of the Marines. We were there to protect them from the Raghead suicide motorboats, which were rumored to be loaded with TNT and aimed at any American ship they could reach. (Author's note: "Ragheads" could be interpreted as a derogatory term applied to anyone who wears some version of middle eastern headgear, but in this case it was shorthand for

Speed brakes deployed, an A-6E (BuNo 161678) of VMA (AW)-332 Polkadots makes its final approach to MCAS Yuma, Arizona, on 18 October 1990. The nose radome appears to have been freshly repainted. (Ted Carlson)

A pair of A-6Es of VA-128 enroute to targets at NAF El Centro, California, on 26 February 1988. They are armed with Mk 82 500 pound Snakeye retarded bombs on MERs. The A-6 in the foreground has an AIM-9 Sidewinder air-to-air missile rail on the inboard pylon. (U.S. Navy by Robert L. Lawson)

the many different factions...almost too numerous and obscure to mention...within Lebanon, who had reason to wish harm to anyone who was trying to restore some semblance of stability to the region). I don't remember any instances of actually being threatened by one of these boats.

We also flew ground support missions for the Marines at Beirut International Airport (BIA) or at the American Embassy. The Marines had FACs at both locations and they would call out possible targets. We were allowed to fly right up to the beach, but not over it, so the Ragheads knew of our presence. We generally carried laser-guided bombs and Rockeye cluster bombs for these missions, and there was always an A-6 airborne with live ordnance during this period. The alert airplanes could provide follow-up within minutes. We also patrolled between the island of Cyprus and the Lebanon coast to keep track of several Soviet ships. If they came south from Syria, the Admiral wanted to know about it as soon as possible.

Our "tattletale" was a Soviet modified KASHIN class guided missile destroyer (mod Kashin), which probably provided the early warning on the day that we struck them, because the Ragheads knew we were coming. Tattletales are pretty much a fact of life for all Med carriers. Our strike in Lebanon was on 3 December 1983. A-6s and A-7s from the USS KENNEDY and USS INDEPENDENCE flew this mission in two waves. CAG Andrews, from INDEPENDENCE, was the first aircraft over the beach. He was flying an A-7 and he was shot down. VA-85 lost an A-6. The A-6 pilot, LT Mark Lange, was killed and the BN, LT Bobby Goodman, wound up a prisoner, although he was later released. The side number of their aircraft was 556.

This strike was a real quick reaction deal. We pulled out of Haifa, Israel on 2 December and flew that afternoon. The next morning, I was awakened at about 0400. One of my duties in the squadron was that of schedule officer, so when they needed crews, I was the first one notified. I was told to get ten crews up and ready. We were given about five minutes to plan, five minutes to brief and ten minutes to get to our aircraft. The ordnancemen were busy changing the loads for our mission. We were given a time on target (TOT) of approximately 0800 and although the Admiral had asked for an extension, it was denied somewhere up the chain of command.

One of our F-14 TARPS reconnaissance aircraft had been fired on, and we were going to show them what would happen if they continued to shoot at our aircraft. Our targets were various gun positions and other known positions of various hostile factions in the civil war. We had never planned for a strike of a large group of airplanes. The tactical advantage of the A-6 is its ability to fly in all weather conditions, but this means flying one or two plane missions. Conducting an "Alpha Strike" resulted in re-learning a lot of the lessons from Vietnam...on short notice. The beneficial fall-out of the mistakes made on this mission was the clockwork success of the mission carried out against Libya a few years later.

The latest low-viz camouflage scheme is carried by this A-6E of VMA (AW)-242 Bats. Under this scheme, aircraft often do not display the unit name or number, but do have the squadron insignia...such as 242's stylized bat. (Sinichi Ohtaki)

An A-6E of VMA (AW)-533 (BuNo 154169) returns from a Red Flag mission at Nellis Air Force Base, Nevada, on 23 August 1989. The aircraft has a sensor pod on the inboard pylon and MERs on the outboard pylons. (Ted Carlson)

We counted a dozen surface-to-air missiles from our cockpit (probably infrared or heat seeking missiles). We were at high altitude which limited the A-6 infrared signature so the missiles didn't have much to lock on to. Every Raghead over there was probably issued one of these things and they filled the sky with them (shoulder launched SA-7s). There was a lot of artillery and they were obviously expecting us to come in low, because we overflew all of it, with the shells bursting several thousand feet below us. We were the last division over the beach, and the A-6 that was shot down was number three in our three plane division, so it was the last aircraft of the entire strike group to ingress. I likened the situation to following someone who has hit a hornet's nest. By the time you get there, the hornets are really pissed! My pilot's comment when we crossed the beach, outbound, said it all, "Now I know how a dove feels on opening day of hunting season!"

We got a new airplane flown over from MATWING in Virginia Beach to replace the one we lost, so we gave it the side number 556. My pilot and I jumped into that airplane on 11 January for a "routine" tanker mission. Our launch was at 0530 from the number one catapult (starboard bow). Although it was still dark, there was a visible horizon and that probably saved our lives. We felt the initial jolt as the catapult fired but we did not feel the acceleration of a normal cat shot. We both knew right away that something was wrong. I yelled for brakes. My pilot stomped on the brakes, chopped the throttles to idle and reached for the emergency/parking brake. Neither of us felt any immediate danger because I think we both thought we would stop. I think that in normal circumstances we probably would have stopped but because we had been conducting around the clock flight ops since the strike, the flight deck was very slippery. This prevented any traction and caused the aircraft to turn slightly to the left. When I saw him reach for the parking brake, I looked outside and saw the edge of the bow approaching. I don't ever remember thinking, "Should I or shouldn't I eject?" I subconsciously determined that if the plane was going to stop, it was going to do so without me in it! My reflexes took over. I told my pilot to get ready and I went for the lower ejection handle. I was looking down as the seat fired, so I saw the rocket motor light off. I blasted through the canopy and into the sky. It seemed like a

relatively smooth ride. I felt the opening shock of the parachute, looked down and saw water. My emergency oxygen was not working so I released one side of my oxygen mask. The next thing I saw was my pilot in his parachute in front of me. I was preparing to go into the water in front of the ship when a gust of wind blew me over the edge of the bow. The next thing I knew, I was being dragged down the deck by my parachute while sitting on my ejection seat pan. Our squadron maintenance troubleshooters who worked the catapult launches reacted quickly and collapsed my parachute. I stopped about the same place I had started just a few seconds before! My pilot's parachute had drifted more to the port side and his chute caught on the deck. When the chute caught, he was swung into the side of the ship and got bruised up pretty badly. He was just hanging there when a couple of alert sailors in the port catwalk found him and hoisted him up. While I was waiting for my pilot, I walked into flight deck control and called our ready room to tell them we were O.K.

It was absolutely amazing that we ejected in the middle of the sea and neither one of us got our feet wet! My injuries were limited to a bruised left arm. I think my bruises came from the center canopy brace on my way out of the aircraft. I was able to fly the next day, but my pilot was down for about three weeks recovering from his injuries. After we lost our second A-6 with the side number 556, our skipper said, "There will be no more 556s in this squadron!" Neither one of us realized how close we had come until the next day when we watched the PLAT video (every launch and recovery is recorded with a low light capable camera). As it turned out, I ejected about a second before our A-6 went over the bow. My pilot ejected just as the starboard main mount was going off the edge which caused him to be shot out in front of me. As we were watching the video, we both looked at each other in muted awe, realizing we were some lucky bubbas to be sitting there!

I had an even closer call several years later during a flight test at the Naval Air Test Center at Patuxent River, Maryland. The A-6 I was flying suffered a catastrophic failure in the longitudinal flight control system (the horizontal stab failed leading edge full up) resulting in an uncontrollable pitch over. The airplane experienced immediate massive negative G forces (approximately -6.4 Gs). I still don't remember much of the events of

The new low-visibility markings mean that even CAG aircraft are often bland! This A-6E of VA-34 at NAS Oceana during November of 1988 is the unit's CAG bird, as identified by the 500 side number. (D.F. Brown)

This KA-6D Intruder tanker of VA-43 carries low visibility camouflage and markings, including subdued air group and squadron markings. (Don Spering via Norman E. Taylor)

This A-6E (BuNo 158045) of VA-176 on the ramp at Shaw AFB, S.C., on 9 November 1988, was assigned to USS FORRESTAL. Even though it is the CAG aircraft, the squadron and carrier markings are so small and subdued that they are nearly invisible. (Norman E. Taylor)

that day. I do remember the unplanned onset of negative G, and saying; "PULL" (meaning pull back on the stick), and reaching like hell for the lower ejection handle. I don't remember pulling the handle, but obviously, I did. Unfortunately, the pilot (our Chief Test Pilot) did not and crashed with the A-6. I ejected at approximately 500 knots, 3,500 feet, 180 degrees inverted and -4 Gs. The ejection was extremely violent. My helmet and oxygen mask were sucked off my head and were later found with my mask still attached on both sides. I broke my lower left tibia, my right hand and shoulder blade, shattered my left humerus, cut up my right ear and had two symmetrical black eyes, probably from the massive negative Gs. I now have a hardware store (three plates and about two dozen screws) in my left arm. The investigation board was able to determine the cause of the accident because flight testing requires that the airplane is highly instrumented. It makes me wonder though how many other A-6s (with aircrews) that disappeared for unknown reasons during carrier ops over the years suffered the same failure.

He was in the hospital for twenty-three days, in a wheelchair for two months and on crutches for another month. He was in physical and occupational therapy five days a week for three months, decreased that to three days a week for the next two months and flew again six and a half months after the accident. When I remarked that it was a dangerous business, he noted that more people died in car accidents than in tactical aircraft accidents. Maybe so, but I would bet that a lot more adrenaline is burned up in jets than in Buicks!

The Libya of COL Khadafi had become one of the worlds leading sponsors of terrorism. Under Khadafi, Libya had become a training ground for terrorists and a regular sponsor of prototypical terrorist attacks against western interests. Ronald Reagan was well aware of Khadafis participation and sponsorship of these activities and he had decided to send Khadafi a message. The message was a coordinated strike against Libyan military targets, using USAF F-111s from England and Navy attack aircraft from carriers in the Gulf of Sidra, operating below Khadafi's so-called "Line of Death." The following are the impressions of one of the A-6 Bombadier Navigators on that mission.

The night sky above the carrier deck was filled with stars and the fresh salt air seemed to soothe my nervousness as my pilot and I searched for our aircraft under the yellow glow of the flight deck flood lights. Above the sound of the ship making its way at high speed to our launch position off the coast of Libya, I could hear the Air Boss notifying all flight deck personnel that aircrews were manning the strike aircraft. The flight deck bustled

This A-6E (BuNo 161662) of VA-85 scored a kill against a Libyan missile boat during March of 1986. The aircraft carried a small kill marking behind the cooling air louvers under the cockpit. (D.F. Brown)

with activity as the aircraft and catapults were made ready. As my eyes adjusted to the darkness, I saw what appeared to be the picture from a Vietnam-era history book — the flight deck was filled with ordnance-laden aircraft. It was an awesome display of firepower.

We were greeted at 502 by an abnormally large number of squadron maintenance personnel, all beaming with enthusiasm and sincere concern for their particular areas of responsibility. Each gave gestures of good luck and a few even lent their lucky charms. I carried one man's camouflage bandana and another man's rabbit foot; hopeful, of course, that I would be able to return each to its rightful owner in a couple of hours. As I preflighted the aircraft and weapons, I couldn't resist adding my own comments to the graffiti covering the bombs. The sayings were not quite suitable for public release, but then again, we were not delivering the Evening News.

To be forced to face one's own mortality — to confront the very real and near term possibility of death — was a gate through which every aircrew passed that evening. Some realized the possible consequences as they were returning to the ship after the mission. Others, including myself, faced the reality of death beforehand. I'll never forget the overwhelming emotion which swept my thoughts as I wrote a letter in my state room to my wife and newborn son. We had our son's delivery induced just three days prior to deployment so I could share in his new life. Then, in the ten minutes I had before manning the aircraft, I had to somehow express in a few short words all the love I felt for them both, and employ her to tell him about me. As I reflect back now to my Libyan experience, one of the greatest differences combat made in my life was forcing me to realize that death was an inherent risk of the job. Through the years I've noticed a difference in the eyes of those who have seen combat and those who have not — those who have had to face combat have had to face death.

Once inside the familiar surroundings of the cockpit, my nervousness and apprehensions were overcome by years of

This A-6E (BuNo 161681) of VA-55, sports a missile boat kill marking and a MiG-23 kill marking on the fuselage under the cockpit. The MiG was killed on the ground at Benina Airfield, near Benghazi, on the night of 15/16 April. (D.F. Brown)

A-6E (BuNo 159317) of VA-55 took part in the raid on Benina Airfield, and sports a MiG-23 kill marking as a result. VA-55 was established on 7 October 1983, and was the Navy's newest Intruder squadron when it went into battle during March/April of 1986, while on their first deployment. (D.F. Brown)

A pair of A-6Es of VA-35 on a practice mission on 10 November 1986. Both aircraft are configured with MERs on the outboard pylons and 300 gallon fuel tanks on the inboard pylons. (U.S. Navy by PH1 Ronald Beno)

An A-6E Intruder of VA-35 on the ramp at NAS Oceana during October of 1987. The squadron was assigned to USS THEODORE ROOSEVELT. The aircraft carries a mix of low-vis markings and full Black numbers and codes. (D.F. Brown)

These A-6Es of VA-36 deployed from NAS Oceana aboard USS THEODORE ROOSEVELT in support of Operation DESERT SHIELD, and were one of the first squadrons to go into combat during DESERT STORM. (Robert F. Dorr)

we were nonetheless thankful to have a horizon reference, as well as some visual cues to aid in our attack. As I watched the missiles fall on the innocent population below, I instantly realized the terrible consequences of war.

At approximately two minutes from the target, I peered out the right windscreen in time to observe the salvo launch of two missiles. Unlike the previous missiles that changed relative bearing quickly as they passed the aircraft, their glare grew in intensity along the same relative bearing. There was only one explanation for the difference —these missiles were guiding on us! "Break right!" I called excitedly. although unaware of the impending danger, the pilot sensed the urgency in my voice and immediately responded. However, feeling uncomfortable in the low altitude right turn at night, the pilot reversed direction after several seconds, and increased the Gs. The cockpit, normally dimly lit by red instrument lights, was suddenly filled with a magnificent white light as the two missiles passed close abeam our airplane. I braced for the warhead detonation...Nothing.

"We beat them." I said confidently. Or had we? The "SAM break" maneuver resulted in two very severe consequences. First, we gained altitude in the maneuver which made us more vulnerable to Libyan air defenses. Several amber caution lights advised us of the second — the inertial navigation system had "dumped" (failed). "Can we make it?" the pilot asked. The A-6 computer bombing solution requires accurate inputs from one of its three navigation modes. However, degrading to the secondary or tertiary modes and then executing an attack with precision accuracy is procedurally cumbersome. The time required to complete the transition and the bombing accuracy obtained in the degraded mode is largely a function of training and proficiency. On this particular night, I was grateful for the intensive training I'd received as a student in the Fleet Replacement Squadron. Hours of degraded system instruction and practice paid dividends as my hands moved swiftly and instinctively. "Yes, we can make it." I responded confidently.

My total attention was focused on locating and identifying the target area and making fine aim point corrections. Arming the weapons system, I informed the pilot, "Master Arm - ON; In ATTACK." As he squeezed the commit trigger and centered the attack steering commands, the pilot responded, "Good symbology, I'm committing." Seconds later, the hammer-shaped symbol that visually indicated the time remaining to release touched the bottom of the pilot's display; release was imminent. Lightened by the shedding of its heavy load, the airplane shuddered noticeably as our bombs began their earthward journey. Through the rearview mirrors in the cockpit we saw the bright orange flashes of our bombs exploding. In that instant, I felt the overwhelming burden of ultimate accountability.

We egressed the target area at high speed and followed the return to force procedures previously briefed. Exiting the high threat area, I was torn with emotion. Part of me wanted to exalt in jubilation, while the other part was still tense; fearful for the safety of my comrades. We listened intently to the radio as each returning Intruder called "Feet Wet." Finally, the last call was made — all squadron aircraft were safe. "Tonight, we changed the course of history," we agreed.

Clearly, the best measure of the success of any effort lies in the result. The strike was thoroughly planned and flawlessly executed, enabling all Navy aircraft to return safely without sustaining any combat damage. But most importantly, the decline in Libyan sponsored worldwide terrorism and specifically the subduing of COL Khadaffi, were apparently achieved. Without a doubt, the Libyan strike of 15 April 1986 established a level of success by which other missions will be measured and paid great tribute to the A-6 Intruder and all the courageous aircrew who have flown it into combat.

Another of the participants described sinking a NANUCHKA Class patrol boat.

There were multiple patrol boats out there and most of the ones that were sunk, were sunk by A-6s because most of the action was at night. The show started when the bad guys shot SA-5 missiles at an A-7. We went in and knocked down the SA-5 sites. That brought the patrol boats out to sea. In the middle of the night, A-6s from VA-85 went in and knocked hell out of them...sunk

This A-6E of VA-36 carries the alternate low-viz squadron markings in Light Gray, but still has the aircraft side number in Black. The equipment bay rack is down for maintenance. (D.F. Brown)

Armed with Mk 20 Rockeye Cluster Bomb Units (CBUs), an A-6E TRAM Intruder is positioned on the number one catapult prior launch. The Mk 20 Rockeye was widely used in DESERT STORM against a variety of targets. (U.S. Navy)

a bunch of boats. The next morning at sunrise, it appeared that everything was over, but the morning launch immediately spotted a NANCHUKA class guided missile patrol boat coming out of Benghazi. (Authors note: The NANCHUKA class boat can carry six SS-N-9 surface-to-surface missiles, which have a range of thirty miles and a potential range, with airborne relay from an aircraft with video data link, of 150 miles). An A-6 from USS CORAL SEA attacked the boat with Rockeyes, spreading them across the fantail and the port side. This attack started a number of fires. Another A-6, again from VA-85, launched a Harpoon missile from about fifteen miles and within ten minutes the Nanuchka sank. All of these attacks were carried out within the SA-2 defensive ring, right off the beach, but no SAMs were launched because the A-6s stayed at 300 feet or lower! The MiGs stayed home too, even though we were pretty close to Benina airfield.

It is probably no accident that COL Khadaffi has maintained such a low profile since this mission. His defenses never laid a glove on the Navy, and the one F-111 which was lost was never recovered, so no one really knows what happened to it. The mission is a testament to the effectiveness of a military force which is allowed to operate with enough autonomy to accomplish the objective without the micro-management which so hampered the military in Vietnam.

The Libyan operation was a precursor to the much larger and more dramatic successes of Operation DESERT STORM. As of this writing, the details of DESERT STORM and the Intruder's role are still coming out. The results are well known...a 1,000 hour war in which the fourth largest army in the world and the sixth largest air force in the world were totally routed and humiliated. Going into the war, it was felt that Iraqi air defense equipment was capable of

VMA (AW) 224 was one of the Marine Corps squadrons which saw combat during DESERT STORM. This A-6E TRAM (BuNo 161666) carries an AIM-9 Sidewinder air-to-air missile on the outboard wing pylon. While the A-6 can carry the Sidewinder, it takes up a pylon that would normally be used for bombs. (Ted Carlson)

inflicting severe casualties on coalition air forces. How would thirty year old attack bombers survive in a totally integrated air defense environment? We know the answer to that question...we just don't have all the details yet. We know that superior training and tactics dispensed with the "force parity" that many experts claimed existed prior to the start of DESERT STORM. And the 30 year old Intruder was proven to still be a viable weapons system.

The official Grumman Intruder logo has been reproduced as a patch and is worn by many A-6 crews.

An A-6E TRAM shares the ramp at a forward airfield somewhere in Saudi Arabia with F/A-18 Hornets during Operation DESERT SHIELD. The Hornets are from a Marine Corps fighter/attack squadron. (USAF)

An A-6E (BuNo 152634) of VA-145 takes off from Nellis AFB, Nevada, during a Red Flag mission on 23 March 1988. The aircraft is carrying three 400 gallon fuel tanks on the underwing pylons. (Ted Carlson)

An EA-6B Prowler moves into position to take on fuel from a USAF KC-135 tanker during Operation DESERT SHIELD. The pace of operations often had U.S. Navy aircraft being refueled by USAF tankers. (USAF)

An A-6E Intruder is refueled by a KC-135 of the Kansas Air National Guard over Saudi Arabia. The Intruder is carrying 300 gallon fuel tanks on the inboard pylons. (USAF)

EA-6B Prowlers of VAQ-130 in company with an F-14 of VF-32 during a DESERT SHIELD mission. The Tomcat is fully armed with AIM-54, AIM-7 and AIM-9 missiles. The probing of Iraqi defenses during DESERT SHIELD resulted in overwhelming success when it came time to suppress those defenses during DESERT STORM. (USAF)

Ground crews load a 2,000 pound Laser Guided Bomb (LGB) onto the inboard wing pylon of a VMA (AW)-224 A-6E Intruder. (USAF)

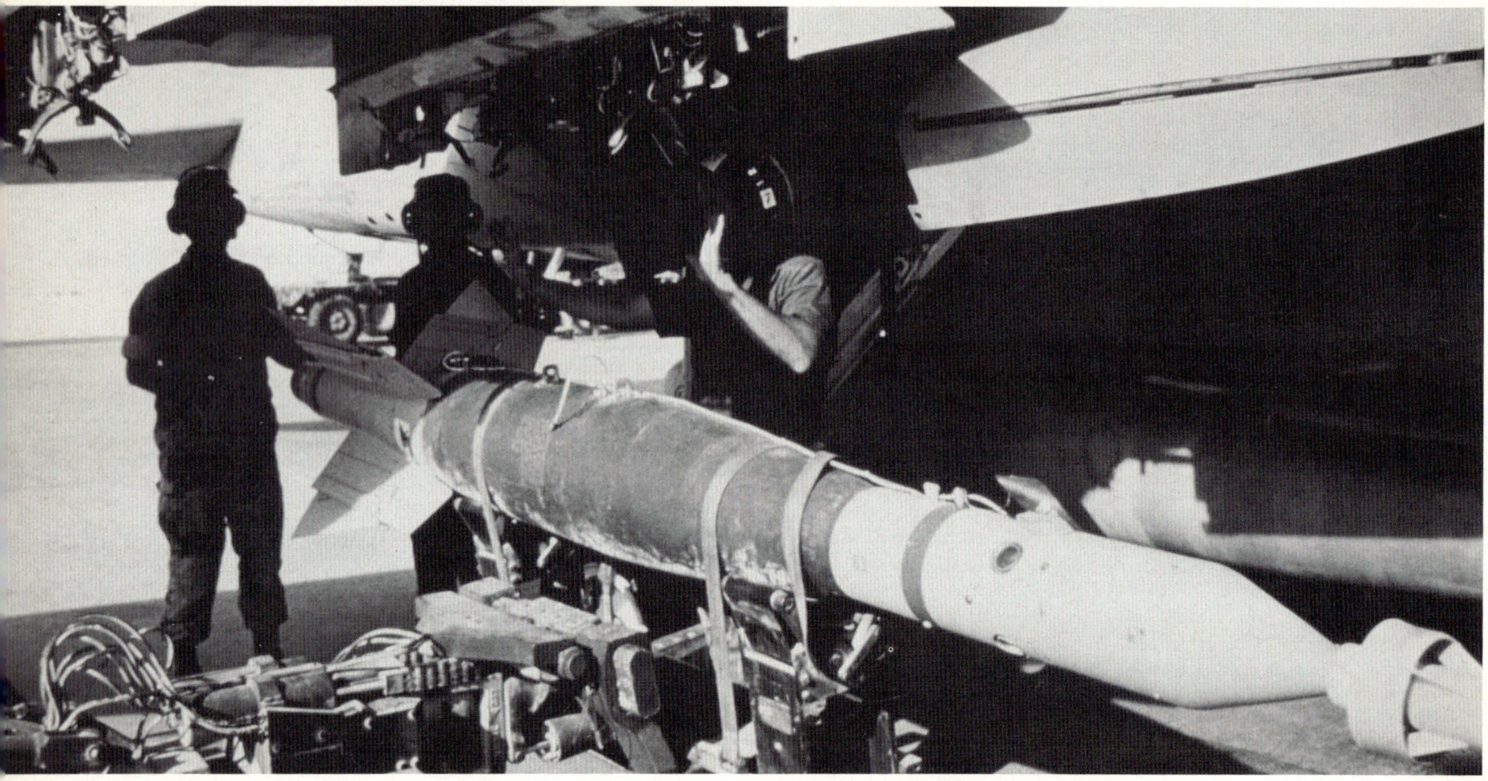

VA-65 also served aboard USS THEODORE ROOSEVELT during Operation DESERT STORM. This A-6E (BuNo 157001) was on the NAS Oceana ramp during early 1990, prior to deployment aboard ROOSEVELT. (Robert F. Dorr)

Marines prepare Mk 20 Rockeye Cluster Bomb Units (CBUs) for loading on VMA (AW)-224 A-6 Intruders. The Intruders operated from Royal Saudi Air Force bases. (USAF)

An A-6E acts as a tanker for a flight of A-7E Corsiar IIs armed with Rockeye CBUs. The Intruder is carrying four 400 gallon fuel tanks and a buddy refueling store on the centerline station (USAF)

An A-6E TRAM enroute to targets in either Kuwait or Iraq with a load of 1,000 pound bombs. The aircraft carries over twenty mission makings on the nose in front of the air intake (USAF)

The company-sponsored attempt to extend the life of the Intruder was the A-6F, which was designed for increased crew survivability, reliability, and maintainability. It differed from the A-6E in that it had a narrower nose, additional outer wing pylon, 10,800 lbst GE F-404 engines, Norden radar and digital avionics. It was first flown during August of 1987, but was later cancelled. (Grumman)

As the A-12 program slipped further behind, it became evident that something would have to be done to extend the life of the A-6. The answer was a new wing, built by Boeing Military Airplanes division of the Boeing Company. The new wing is a Graphite/epoxy composite with titanium used in areas of high stress along with a nickle-coated fabric to provide protection from lightning strikes. (Boeing)

The new wing was estimated to add 8,800 flight hours, or about 15 years, to the operational life of the A-6. First flight of the composite wing took place on 3 April 1989. The composite wing is stronger than the original wing and more resistant to corrosion. (Boeing)